MEMOIRS OF A HIGH SCHOOL SNEAKER PIMP...
FICTION WITH A FEW AUTOGRAPHS

BY ETERNAL AKASA-RA BAKR

Memoirs of a High School Sneaker Pimp…Fiction with a few Autographs

Copyright © 2019 Yellow Kicks, LLC

All rights reserved. This book, or parts thereof, may not be used, utilized or reproduced in any manner whatsoever without the written permission of the copyright owner except for the use of quotations in a book review.

For publisher information, address:

Yellow Kicks, LLC

eternal@yellowkicks.com

sneakerpimpbook@gmail.com

First paperback edition March 2019

Front cover: Design and illustrations by Darian "Fontana" Logan
Darian.logan@gmail.com

Back cover: Graphics and illustration by Titus V. Thomas
www.TitusCanDraw.com
Photography: Billy Williams
www.unsplash.com

ISBN: 978-0-615-29481-0 (paperback)

ISBN: 978-0-578-43584-8 (ebook)

www.HighSchoolSneakers.com

Disclaimer

Even though subtitled "Fiction with a few Autographs", this book is indeed based on my high school experience, not to be confused with inspired by. For me, the term Autographs was a play on words and meanings. It was my abbreviated definition for autobiography as well as a signature of personal highlights. So yes, in truth, this work is not fiction at all. And if I wasn't so cocky when I wrote the book I probably wouldn't have subtitled it in the first place, but here we are. The only part that is actually fiction is filler information. Anything that seems mundane is fabricated for fluidity. Anything that seems outlandish is totally true. If you don't believe me, find one of my old high school friends. All character names have been changed for obvious reasons. Samyra, you know who you are. Let's make that scene happen. (This will make sense after reading chapter 7, except for the eating box part. Never been a boxer!)

This book is dedicated to the living memory of my brother, Orion, my sister, Blossom, my father, Abu Bakr and my grandmother, June Murray. May you guys rest in peace, in the sanctuary of my mind.

Honorable Mention

Ty! My celestial twin. What up homie? If not for you, this idea would have never materialized. It was you and I in Kazi's old house on Sterling Place, talking that fly lingo that only international sneaker pimps talk. We both said we had a dope book idea. If memory serves me correctly, I only added the "High School" and "Memoirs" part to the title and of course the ambiguous subtitle. We sucked at writing together because we always ended up talking more about our stories then actually jotting them down. This pen is still in your honor. To my older brothers, for placing my perspective in a kaleidoscope. You guys gave me a tour of the landscape, showing me everything from hood boogers to empresses (this is probably the first time in history that hood booger and empress were put in the same sentence). Ta, I remember when you were breaking up with Pam. As she pulled up to the house, I was sitting on the stoop with you, Ade from upstairs and some friends. She was at least ten years your senior. She came out the car and unzipped her pants in broad daylight, slapped her crotch and said, "What's wrong. You too good for this now?" The take away for me; insanity doesn't care about the public or broad daylight.

To Farah, my cult tester, thank you for understanding me and my complicated yet simplistic vision, and for giving me every womanly emotion associated with each and every chapter. You represent intellectual women rock stars everywhere. I remember us walking into some ultra-euro boutique in The Village, on Bleecker Street to be exact. We were both looking at clothes. Not really shopping, just being young and hip. You saw something you liked. You tried it on, came out of the dressing room, called me over and asked, "Do my breast look really big in this?" "Yup." We been super homies ever since.

I can't forget to thank my mother and father, because who doesn't thank their parents when on a podium? And last but not least I want to send an extra special thanks to each and every woman who has graced my life with their presence. My lessons were well "learnt."

To my Sneaker Pimps

The thirst was real; fashion was an addiction supplied by many dealers. The only thing better than an exclusive pair of kicks were those same kicks in a new colorway. It was a cultural phenomenon. For urban footwear, the 1990s were truly a renaissance period. In my era, young kings and queens wore blinged-out crowns, on their feet.

If you are asking what could possibly top a young man's obsession with Hip Hop music, fresh gear and exclusive kicks with the new colorway? There was only one answer:

Girls!

Girls!

Girls!

Girls!

Introduction

This wasn't a loose hobby of mine. There was structure behind my views. It's really a science and the artistry lies within the finesse of this science. One plus one will always equal two, but blue plus yellow will give you many variations of green. It all depends on the input. It all depends on your style.

There were a few times in my life when one particular girl would constantly call my house. She probably was a girl I showed the most interest in, at the moment. Since my mother would often answer the ring (her phone bill, technically her phone), she had a mental record of the female friends who would call. She once asked me, "Who is Tonya? Are you getting serious with this girl?" To which my honest reply was, "No, she's just another cool chick who is open off your son. Can you blame them?" I would say that jokingly while flexing in the mirror to show mom-dukes that push-ups really work. She would say, "I don't want you getting caught up with one girl. You're young. Enjoy yourself—not too much but experience life."

Now as a young adolescent male, there were many ways to take that. I, of course, took it as the ultimate authorization and endorsement to run amok with the blessings of my own mother. She really didn't mean for me to play mind games or take girls on emotional roller coaster rides. "Don't lead them on. Be honest but don't get trapped up." This came from a woman who counseled so many relationships that she should've been given an honorary degree in the field. So it definitely carried some weight with me. The jewel she was trying bestow upon me was the value of exploration and the fact that I might want to look in different gardens if I want to find different bugs. Thanks, Lady.

My mother was sharp. She knew why she spoke and at the same time why she listened. She had an uncanny way of making someone's words seem important even if they weren't. My mother was warm and comforting. I slowly acquired this same ability to generate warmth. My older brothers, through demonstration, showed me how to refine that quality by placing some of that warmth in the deep freeze.

Some say the developing signs of social behavior can be readily noted as early as preschool (on the playground). But, when is this behavior calcified? At what point, does what you do become who you are? I believe high school hones our character—the watering hole of adolescent social equality, or the lack thereof. The marketplace for one's values, bonds, aspirations and insecurities are all present in the high school setting. They remain throughout life—just modified. Thereafter, the root remains the same. In most cases, high school will serve as a microcosm to the rest of your adult relations.

There are many social worlds intertwined in this institutional setting. As a developing teen, it serves best to be well versed in as many as possible. This memoir focuses on one world—mine—and the way my learned behavior was modified for my desire to be psychologically and incomparably dominant in the courting process. Whoa! That actually sounds pretty selfish with the absence of all feelings except my own. Let me rephrase that. This memoir is about the psyche of a young man in the presence of typical situations provoking untypical reactions, his organic approach to the opposite sex. Ahhh yes! That feels better.

I could lie and say the road I traveled was an easy one. I could say that girls found me irresistible—instantly; that I was born with the gift of gab and that every word from my mouth was witty, intelligent or even provocative. I could say that I came from a pillow of wealth and with the assistance of two silver spoons everything was at my beck and call. My story would actually sound better as a "how to" or "this could be you" fairy tale—but let me be real.

I wasn't given knighthood by an ex-pimp with a splintered cane. My heart wasn't broken into so many pieces that when I put it back together I was a completely different person, seeking revenge or some story-like vendetta. My background wasn't extraordinary or tragic. Family friction hadn't brazed my skin. I wasn't a lone wolf. So many older brothers, a best friend down the block, more friends across the street, two older cousins and a godfather's frequent visits and pickups kept my baby blue hue navy. My parents were married for 18 years before they separated. I was the youngest boy in the household, maybe around 12 when he moved out. Surprisingly though, there was no emotional void after my father left. And that wasn't because we lacked a close relationship or the love wasn't there. The saying holds true, it does take a village. In my case, the village was male dominant. The general leaving to establish another post is less worrisome when the captains follow the same creed.

My father's principles and the actions that comprised his aura were innate to my makeup. His lessons I absorbed vicariously. I'm not sure how my father gathered his lessons though. We never got around to that. But for me, it was observation. You'll be surprised by what silence can teach you. And when something was missed by my juvenile eye, one of my brothers were there to deliver the day's lesson. It was never about the chef and always about the meal. It wasn't who fed me—it was the fact that I ate. This buffet-style of nourishment gave me many options—many outfits in a seasonal, yet fashionable world. Make no mistake about it, some people do things just because they can and I felt like the guy with the chainsaw in his juggling act. Who juggles a chainsaw? The person who can.

At the age of 15, I remember telling my academic peers, "Don't hate the game baby! Hate the rules." Looking back, boy was that insightful. We all played under guidelines, but whose guidelines and could they be changed? At first I wanted to be a player, and untuck my jersey. Then a team owner, where my Super 180's, distressed oxfords and Windsor knot could do the talking for me. That's a suit, shoe and tie reference. Eventually I just wanted to be a stadium—that way, I win no matter who's playing. Let them play themselves. Home team or away, same difference to the scoreboard. If I walk in expecting nothing, how can I ever be disappointed in my encounters? This was a transitional period of thinking for me. I had an out-of-body experience to watch these thoughts blossom. This made me even more detached from the soft stuff.

Girls would ask, "Where are your emotions? You seem so cold hearted. Do you even have any?" To which I would reply, "Of course, they are neatly folded in my drawer over there. I just don't have time to wear them." An intelligent answer for everything—got that one from my pops. Being on point promotes business at cocktail parties. It can save lives at wartime. It could even get you an "A" on a "B" paper (but that's another story). I started studying people and their reactions at an early age. In so doing, I learned how to provoke the responses of girls. It entertained me. It challenged my natural prowess and gave this cat a post on which to sharpen his claws. It was love at first strike. Every person prepared me for the next. I went for the head. Swinging my proverbial sword at an obstacle only made me stronger (The Highlander).

Along with the slight stitching of my father's vanity genes, the jewels that were bestowed upon me contributed to my flashiness—but this flash was always displayed with a just bit of humility. A wise man once told me, "Accessories are like icing. Without the cake, how many people just want icing?" Actually, it was me who came up with that (Humility anyone?) and I could answer it too just to play devil's advocate: The same people who take whip cream to the head—hungry people with nothing left in the fridge except for baking soda and left over icing from a homemade birthday cake, but I totally understand that wise man's point. He makes sense. Despite all the makeup this world has to offer, when you get home and slip from your outerwear and face that gorgeous mirror in which you admire, what's the cake made of? What are your ingredients? And if you don't like those ingredients, can you change them before your character is baked in? Just remember, if the icing made the cake, the cake wasn't that special to begin with.

I was once asked if I thought I had good luck with women. The straight answer: No! There is a huge difference between a kid with a machine gun and a marksman with a rifle. Precision and calculation is the North Star, not adrenaline and good fortune. All that, just to say this wasn't a loose hobby of mine. Asking a child to write with their left hand not knowing they are ambidextrous is sort of how I felt while talking with girls—my friends were impressed with the boldness but it was natural occurrence. This pursuit was woven into my personality.

I didn't become who I am with the intention of teaching others. But let's face it, with any great accumulation of knowledge comes an evitable role as mentor that one should hopefully accept. I have accepted this charge, and I am obliged to reveal the concealed—or better stated, the illusion of it. Let me explain.

The intricacies of a woman? Yup! A statement and question all in one. Pay attention to the details. Within the context of casual conversation, I found myself learning everything I've ever wanted to know about the girl in front of me. No need to dig when the landscape is an open forum. Body language and small facial quirks, that's the key. Not to mention the ability to detect acute temperature changes, kept me aware of whether I was hot or cold in my efforts. To the observer goes the spoils. I started off as a good listener. A really, really good listener. To my lady sneaker pimps, everything written above and below applies to him too.

If you want to learn about the world? Start analyzing relationships. It really is universal, u-n-i-verse. You and I verse, get it? Simply put, we take turns—but in so doing, we may create avenues not essential to communication. The reaction to stimuli, blinded by tradition often separates what a man thinks he should do from what he does. Modern linguistics and semantics shield what he says from what he means. The language barrier occurs most often within one's own language and not between them. In high school, the quickest way from point A to point B is whatever line works. Ha!

"So, how is this done?" you might ask. What is the common denominator that provides both the floundering wordplay of the novice and the nuanced wit of the astute favorable results? In short, us. We are all social beings by nature. The law of attraction is no secret to our makeup. Everything we see is based on a bond, everything. Just like the certainty of taxes and death, appeal is sure to open your eyes. Your eyes want something to look at. Your mouth wants something to say, your nose to smell, your ears to hear and the soul of you just wants something to feel (feel - touch - vibes - vibrations tuned - waves = frequency).

You don't need to tell her everything she wants to hear—even though that approach does work, it is misleading and deceiving. Morality doesn't have to be bland though. Adding a hint of romance, a dash of mystique and a touch of color to your language enhances the experience of someone knowing you. It's the difference between cooking and cooking with your foot in it—no one is searching for the recipe to the former. Excluding sociopaths, you have to like something. You will like someone. If you didn't, why would you even wake up? Excitement and fulfillment are why. Potential is the only promise that hope and tomorrow remain monogamous. Why do we care? What does this all mean?

It's simple. It means I know what I want. I am a predator, an aggressor, actively passive and passively acting, cool, calm and assured. I am concerned with the outcome, for my ego, professionalism and for the forgone stories. These are my lessons, my plans; tailored for the goal. These are the Memoirs of a High School Sneaker Pimp, Fiction with A Few Autographs.

"If we can be attracted to another person, can't our souls be attracted to another soul? If we can be attracted to multiple people simultaneously, can't our souls be attracted to multiple souls simultaneously? IF you agreed to the above statements THEN I have just disproved singular soul mates. Who's down for a spiritual orgy?"

- Efucius

Chapter 1

"She's gonna jump!" someone screamed. I couldn't seem to pinpoint from where the voice originated but I soon realized why it originated. There, about nine stories in the air, I could see a figure. I couldn't see wings but it definitely looked heavenly. As she approached the edge of the building, her eyes widened, overlooking her fifteen minutes of fame. It occurred to me that the crowd, this mosaic abstract of faces, were not her fans. They resembled false hope and empty promises. I could hear her speaking but could not make out the words. Then in the time it took me to squint my eyes in concentration, she was right in front of me or I was right in front of her because now we both stood on the ledge. I placed my pointer and thumb on the bend of her arm, you know that place where nurses misplace needles.

I could feel her pulse racing. I could feel her thoughts. I could feel the sorrow that ran through her veins and emptied over an already drowning heart. She was clearly in despair. As she turned toward me her mouth slowly opened. Carefully and formulated she spoke softly:

ETERNAL BAKR

"My ears are wet. I sleep on my back every night and in this time my tears look for sanity. They roll across my face in search of expression. They seek out my ears hoping for a compassionate welcome, but I can't hear them. It's just too many. I used to cry standing but my mouth couldn't take the bitter taste—a cup of feelings that I forced upon my palate just to keep it wet. A life without guidance is like a baby without a face. I can't face myself because I can't see my future."

With every word spoken she narrowed the distance between herself and the edge. And as if to gesture her last rationale for living, she leaned back, and the soft touch that I had placed earlier on her arm quickly transformed into a grip that caged her innocent wrist. My grip was now her lifeline. Amidst the confusion our eyes met. I knew there, at that very moment, she was listening and before our attention could be divided, I spoke to her:

"Love. The reason you can't see your future is because your sights lie in the wrong direction. You are not the faceless child. You need no labels, no titles, no confirmation of acceptance. You have matured into your existence and need not the promise and care of a contemporary world. You CAN see yourself if you look from within. You are a classic with no rendition and to take this leap you will condemn more than yourself to mornings absent the sun and nights absent the stars. You will have denied a star the space in which to shine and the earth would never ever be the same again. Come with me."

She braced her weight against the gargoyle-like statue that decorated the building on which we stood. Her look of worry gradually changed into a smile. When she attempted to speak, all I could hear was the sound of a bell ringing. Every word she spoke echoed with the ringing of the bell.

MEMOIRS OF A HIGH SCHOOL SNEAKER PIMP

At this point, I was very confused. That mosaic crowd soon turned into recognizable classmates. The grip placed on her wrist was actually me wrinkling my lambskin wallet. Soon she vanished as the fluorescent light robbed me of her history. That bell woke me. I was in the back of my Spanish class, sleeping again. Mr. Gutierrez's accent was so heavy that listening to the lesson was pointless. I always got the notes after class from Rachel or Vanessa anyway (Black/Graphite/Hyper-White Jason Kidds and White/Black Air More Uptempo a.k.a. Scottie Pippen's with the big air on the side). It just depended on which one I felt like flirting with. This time it was Vanessa. Her penmanship was very reader-friendly and bubbly just like her attitude.

As we left the classroom I spoke to her with my arm casually draped over her shoulder. From a distance, it looked as if we were good friends. I told her things like, "I saw your last test scores in Spanish. It might be helpful for you to come to my house later and sleep with me. Nah, seriously! You've seen my recent scores. You have to admit they're impressive. Well, the same way I sleep during class is the same way I sleep at home. So, in a weird way, if you slept with me you might be able to learn more. It's worth a shot!"

She knew I was kidding. But after statements like that, I would give her a certain look as if to say "You know I'm just playing girl, unless you gonna do it." This made our relationship entertaining because I would indirectly hit on her every time we spoke. But I never gave her enough ammo to confide in her friends about my intentions. She couldn't explain to her friends a relationship that she, herself, didn't understand. This was exactly how I liked it.

ETERNAL BAKR

I'd known Vanessa for about three years. We actually attended the same junior high and somehow always had a class together. I would often sit behind her, that way if and when we were caught talking, the teacher would only see Vanessa turned around and me looking ahead. I was just as concerned with my grades as I was with my social life. So, for any girl I approached, who was into her books, me knowing the answers to the "Do Now" assignment wouldn't hurt my objective.

"Aight Nestlé! Take it easy. I'll sleep with you tomorrow," I said as we parted ways. Vanessa became quite fond of her nickname. I didn't give her the name Nestlé because she was dark-skinned or sweet. It just popped in my head as a cool tag. She was dark-skinned and sweet though. Every girl I met was given a nickname. Most would never know they had a tag, but once in a while, if a girl was cool enough and not in harm's way, I would give her the privilege of knowing hers.

Why nicknames? We stylized everything. With a student population of about 4,500, there were just too many *governments* to remember. Case in point: I was telling my boy about Stacy and how she paid for my cab at two in the morning and snuck me in her grandmother's apartment. To which my boy asked, "Which Stacy?" "Hawaii," I replied. She was given the name Hawaii because at one point in high school I went through a phase where I wore a lot of Hawaiian shirts and she seemed to like them a lot, she commented on my splashy shirts whenever the opportunity presented itself. Most names had a story behind them. Others were just spontaneous and funny.

It was a quick way to identify someone without giving a full police description. It also gave us the option to speak about girls in front of others without having to lower our voices. I once gave a girl the name "Bagel Face Mummy." Her face did resemble the dry-eyed look of a mummy but did anything about her remind me of a bagel? I don't even remember—it was just funny as hell whenever my friends or I would say it, "Bagel Face Mummy".

Enough about that, that was just an eighth-period Spanish class which lasted for 51 minutes and what seemed like a Frasier Crane dream—so you know where I'm headed now. It was time to get the hell out of there. And for some reason, I was in the mood for cereal. As usual, everyone was in the hallway chatting with chums while fiddling with their combination locks.

Most of these conversations were long forgotten before anyone ever reached the sidewalk. Some of my so-called peers looked like they should still be in junior high: running up and down the halls, throwing paper balls, playing tag and talking so loud that you might think the person listening needed a hearing aid. "She's right next to you," I would say with a low voice as I passed small clusters of freshmen whose octave levels reminded me of morning show disc jockeys.

Making my way down the hall towards the exit was like leaving a team huddle. I knew just about everyone, from the cool crowd, to the jocks, nerds, bullies, bums, transfer students, and even the shy kid who thought no one knew that her older brother was a super senior. Because of this, I just left my hand extended, giving daps, pounds, bounces, handshakes and the occasional black power fist to familiar faces in the distance. On this particular day, I noticed Amina standing in front of the main entrance talking with a group of girls from the track team.

Amina (Sunkist Orange ACG Wildwood) was about 5'7, 112 lbs.; one of the few girls who could make corduroy pants and turtlenecks look sexy.

ETERNAL BAKR

Amina had these brown eyes that were accentuated by her almond tinted mascara (not that I am a big makeup man but if it looks good, it looks good). She had one of those short spacey cuts that looked like she was auditioning for a role on the Jetsons (her head was just the right size for that cut too). She also had skin that resembled chocolate silk. It could have been water, omega 3 fatty acids or just good genes; either way, her package was presentable and appeased the eye. I walked right into the middle of the group and deliberately interrupted their conversation.

"Amina, we've never been formally introduced. Soooo, I just wanted to acknowledge you and I hope that when time permits we can rap for a bit." When speaking to her I made sure to put the emphasis on *I* and *you*. I stared straight into her eyes as if her friends did not exist. And just like that I broke the gaze and went on my merry way.

Never did I formally introduce myself. Time did not permit and she just happened to be in the direction I was traveling. I figured I'd plant the seed then because I would want to harvest it later. As I walked away, I could see one of the girls in the group look at Amina with the expression of "Damn!" Not "Damn he's fine," but "Damn, what just happened? Who does that?"

The real destination was my house and the objective was April (Sport-Red/Heather Gray Saucony Originals). April was hot on the low, not really fly, not really popular. If you've ever seen a TV show where they made the shy nerdy girl look hot by taking off her glasses, letting down her hair, adding some make-up and shortening her skirt, you'll know what I am talking about. In actuality, she had always been attractive. She just didn't know it and hadn't exploited it yet. Her parents were super strict. Once she was in the house they weren't letting her out. She had to squeeze me in before she was expected home.

Sometimes you have to seize the moment. I was respectful too. I wouldn't keep her long and I would always try to help her with timing and excuses. If it grew later than expected she would tell her dad that there was a sick passenger on the train or something of that nature. April was sheltered as a child. Her first-generation immigrant parents were exposed to many hardships as a young couple and agreed that their first born would be better off shielded from the outside world; in the hopes that she wouldn't become contaminated. April wasn't even allowed to view regular television programs. "Did you catch that special on Komodo dragons last night on PBS?" she once asked. "No I didn't catch that special on Komodo dragons last night on PBS," was my response.

As we all know, one of the biggest problems with putting kids on a short leash is that when you take them out to the park and let them loose, they are liable to run everywhere, sniffing everything. They might also feel betrayed because in their parents' attempts to keep them out of the dirt they've denied them the chance to smell the flowers and even pick a berry or two. April was never exposed to any viruses; therefore, she couldn't adequately develop any form of immunity. I knew sooner or later someone would capitalize on her naive sense of bliss.

So, if you are wondering, no, I didn't turn her out—well, not intentionally. She was a good girl, in every sense of the word—was. Whenever she had a glimpse of freedom she drowned herself in it, so I played the role of a lifeguard. Breathe…one-one-thousand, two-one-thousand, three-one-thousand, breathe! We're gonna need a medic over here, this girl is stuck in a tizzy! For April, every word I uttered was straight crack, penetrating each orifice on its way to her brain where a complete system shutdown was anticipated. Here is an example of one of our cocaine-conversations. Hold on, you might want to sit for this one.

ETERNAL BAKR

Let me give you the proper setting first. She finally visited after all of my coercing.

The setting: My bedroom, which was actually a living room on the garden floor. My last bedroom was so small that I slept on the top half of a bunk bed that had my dresser on it as well. Yes, my dresser was on the mattress with me. If you can picture it, I slept diagonally with my feet dangling off the side of the mattress every night (it wasn't always that bizarre but that's a different story). My mother felt so bad about the setup, she promised me, when the family moved, I could have first pick at room selection, ANY room. I chose the biggest room in that Brownstone and transformed it into my bedroom. Dark honey wood floors, plenty of woodwork and a fireplace. Felt like I was living out the theme music from the Jeffersons, "Movin on up".

A long mirror centered the main wall of the room. On the opposing wall, pictures of landscapes and subjects. (At that time I was a self-proclaimed photographer.) A couch was positioned on a slant facing the television. Behind the couch was one of those knock-off Ming dynasty room dividers sectioning off my bed from the rest of the room. After listening to a few songs and making innocent advances:

Me: "If I do anything that upsets you, please let me know. My mother spent too much time instilling discipline in me for me not to be the gentleman she raised."
April: "No, it's not that. I just don't want to rush things. I mean, I really do like you, but it is my first time."
Me: "Look at my lips and listen to my eyes. Do you think that I could be intimate with you and not talk to you anymore? We do share a homeroom class. That would be some real callous shit to do. I couldn't do that even if I wanted to. I'm not built like that. And in regard to your first time,

there are two ways you can do this. 1. Find the guy you like, fall in love, put your favorite Tevin Campbell or Carl Thomas song on, light a vanilla scented candle and hope that he isn't too rough. Stay in love, break up for whatever potential reason while you are still in love, then emotionally try to place something where your heart once was while it's still in the service department being mended. Notice, after service, it's gonna function a little differently. Or, 2. You can find someone who is cooler than frozen vegetables (She smiles at this point). A person who you respect, a friend who will coach you through the process, someone who will allow you to become a woman and be yourself, all while not leaving the huge emotional burden that comes with your 'first' (I know damn well, though a smaller chance, there is still a chance for her to be emotionally attached to the friend she submits to, as opposed to the boyfriend she submits to, but she doesn't). And it doesn't even have to be me. I just think it might be better for you to find someone you like and are cool with, rather than head over heels for."

Tick...tock...tick...tock………...tick.

Without getting too graphic, from that day on, April became my official side-slide. I wasn't the one asking her to come by my house anymore. It wasn't me telling her which friends to use as alibis for the week. I wasn't even requesting that freaky *Banned from TV* shit. Another teen turned fiend, turned junkie, and I was just your local pusher man trying to keep a client happy. Our routine had become so routine that talking would've only upset timing.

By the time I reached home she would be waiting on my stoop with a smile that would make Mr. Kool Aid jealous. She was totally juiced (pun intended). Oh, yeah, and she was wearing a pair of Jelly Bean Blue and

ETERNAL BAKR

Flamingo Pink Low-Top Dunks when she came. Staying cool and collected I wouldn't even give her a hug—well not yet anyway. She would follow my lead by entering into a clean room. The first thing to be aroused was her sense of smell; aromatherapy was usually my first line of offense. If I knew I was expecting company, I would borrow something from my mother's Body Splash collection. I can't remember the excuse I gave my mother for the frequent favors but she didn't seem to mind as long as I didn't empty her favorites. After squirting my room to death and closing the doors before going to school, April wouldn't be able to tell whether she was on an exotic island or the botanical gardens. That's from an eyes closed perspective of course.

On this day, my mother happened to be doing something in the kitchen, which was right outside of my room door. "Hey Ma! How were your soaps? Who me? My day was great. I just realized that if you sneak into the teachers' cafeteria they look and talk like big students. You can even tell the cool ones from the loners." Speaking in run-on sentences, I wouldn't give her a chance to respond. She chuckled. She was used to my sarcastic monologues after school. "I want you to meet April. She's attracted to my brain. Actually, we go to the same school. She's just gonna be here for a second then she has to get home before her dad shows her which country makes the best belts."

"You shouldn't say that," my mom said, "Well it's nice to meet you too April. I hope to see you again." As we walked back into my room I was sure to leave my door wide open. I had just done two very strategic things. I introduced April to my mother, not because I thought my mother needed to know her. But if any sounds escaped my room my mother wouldn't be thinking "Who's that?" She would have already been acquainted with the company. Next, the act of leaving my room door wide open gave the impression that we couldn't be doing anything. And realistically, who would do anything with their mother in the next room and their door wide open? I would! And for my acquainted fiend, it added to her high. So, there it was: sex-capades in my mother's presence. It was like selling drugs in a police precinct—detrimentally risky, but it gave me a great story to tell my friends if I survived. After our rendezvous, she would quickly make haste and I was off to the next challenge.

That particular evening, I wanted to tidy up. I needed to simplify my team roster. You could love the game but if you don't love the players, why attend practice? At the end of spring's academic semester, I walked around with a piece of paper that read "Name & Number." I approached every girl that I found attractive and said, "Wuts good?! I wanna keep in contact with you. It's for my records. It's gonna be a long summer and I think you're someone I need to know."

The first responses I received felt like a hard sell, not much traction. So, I started to request numbers from girls I knew liked me. Once the other spectators saw how many numbers were collected (especially from girls they personally knew), they started signing that paper like I was an upperclassman with a yearbook. When the day was finally over that piece of loose leaf looked like a legislative petition. I impressed myself with the effectiveness of this approach.

This was the only way that I could see three or four girls standing together that I liked and obtain all of their numbers at the same time without them looking at me suspiciously. For the ones I didn't pursue in the summer, the next school year was like hitting the ground running—running with options, that is. After April left, I wanted to take the time to transcribe those names into my little black book.

I know, a black book. What a cliché—but at one point, we all had one. My book housed four bits of information: the name, the number, the number of people so far (April was probably the 61st entry) and a brief reminder of where I meet them (e.g., Kim-school, Kim-Bronx, Kim-fashion show, Kim-125th Street train station), and on the rare occasion, a question mark, which is pretty self-explanatory.

During my petition phase, I must have accumulated about 255 numbers. There were at least 120-150 girls that I never got around to calling. Those names were never forgotten; they just weren't explored. They all served as flashbacks to interesting moments in time. After a few reminiscing moments, the transfer was complete. I then placed the petition in my bottom drawer. I always kept the original copies for reference.

I started off like everyone else, with a Bic pen and a ripped piece of paper. After that I moved on to using gold pens. I knew a booster in ATL. (Booster: n. a person who steals items from retail stores and resells them on the street, usually at a substantial discount. Who really wanted to spend or even had $300 for a P Wing or $600 for a 92 Ski jacket anyway?) Digital phone books were next and then I just evolved to walking around with a tape recorder and capturing the action live. The maturation. The fellas loved it. Even if I didn't get the number, the live conversation was entertaining enough. Ok, that was a digression.

With a new story etched on my belt and a workable Rolodex, I was ready for more space invasion. Space Invasion is the ability to enter one's mind consciously and subconsciously alike, invading space with ticking time bombs that should work in your favor if secured properly in the vacant mind of your listener.

MEMOIRS OF A HIGH SCHOOL SNEAKER PIMP

So, you are discussing your favorite movie and you mention how you love maple syrup on your blueberry waffles. While going over homework you bring up the sweetest thing you have ever done for your mother. The easiest way to understand this Space Invasion concept is to think how a *Gold Digger* might indirectly mention to her *John* a stressful bill or the worn strap on her favorite clutch. He might end up paying that bill. She might end up with a new bag. Don't get it confused. This cat wasn't looking for a fancy feast. The game has always been cerebral and the love is still for the sport.

Chapter 2

Wheels spinning, rigid tires, my back slanted for speed, the increasing descent chases the horizon. Pricks from thorny branches—suppressed by the purpose of my adrenal glands. Reminds me of the misfortune of my attire. I should have worn long sleeves. My internal GPS suggests my first thoughts of direction. Swiftly, I cut through the brush to welcome the heightened sense of awareness that accompanies danger—only to be reminded of the company that trails me. I pedal hard, I pedal fast. Faster!

Faster! Faster is always slower when your imagination surpasses your ability. Because of that, I can't stop. Propelled by my own determination, I glance behind me. I see nothing. History has dissolved. The oak stump that I passed a split second ago is no more. The squirrels that evaded my dangling leg when I attempted to regain balance almost lost on the uneven terrain have vanished. But the singing bird behind my shoulder is still there. Her song has been muted by the pace of my zealous intentions—the beauty of her voice, sacrificed by my ambition. In my attempts to make time, I am missing it. It's ironic when you start to miss what you prepare for most.

Speaking of missing, I had just missed my alarm. Engulfed in my half dream-like state (which happened way too often) I muddled out of bed. I walked frantically about twelve feet to my alarm and hit the seven-minute snooze. Then back to bed. To my comfy spot. I did this several times every morning. People think its nuts, especially any family member who has crashed in my room for a night or two. I'm often asked, "Why don't you just set your alarm thirty minutes later and get up once?" But in my bizarre head, doing what I do lets me sleep with the preparation of waking rather than letting the morning surprise me. I've grown so accustomed to it that if I try to set my alarm for later, I would make the snooze occur in smaller increments and repeat the whole process. Yup! I'm almost clinical.

Fresh out the shower, no need to shave because I hardly had any facial hair. Not unless you count peach fuzz or the one whisker that I accidentally pulled out in music class while in my *Thinking Man* pose. I jumped right into a pre-ironed wardrobe and was off. Strangely enough, we creased everything. On my walk to school, I noticed two familiar groups ahead of me; my boys and a few senior girls. I could talk with my boys anytime, so I walked right past them without even turning my head but I did raise one hand in the air to form a peace sign (both fingers together). By the chuckles, I assumed they acknowledged my gesture.

A few more yards then, "Good morning ladies. I would offer to carry someone's books but you all look like independent women to me, so I bid you adieu." "Wait!" a girl in the group shouts out, "Why? How does your shirt have a Hilfiger and Polo sign?" "It's called a prototype. I got it from the future," I answered. "Really! And you have to be sarcastic too?" she asked. "Because it's morning, and in the future, sarcastic is the new sexy," I replied. The shirt was actually Frankensteined by me in my creative stage switching around patches. It did help that along with my mother's many occupations, a seamstress was one.

I accompanied the girls on the way to school. It was your typical Thursday. Excitement filled the air, tomorrow's promise of the last day of servitude before the timely break of the glorious weekend could be seen on all faces. Teachers seemed more talkative to other teachers. The Dean was joshing more than usual with unruly students and if you really paid attention you could hear Mr. Cook, the school janitor, hum-singing Al Green's *Love and Happiness*. (Hum-singing: v. that's where you sing a song till you get to the part where you can't remember the lyrics and then hum the rest of the melody.) Everything was well. At least that's what I thought until I was handed a "C" on my trigonometry exam. "What the hell!"

Mrs. Hayes (Light Pink Jil Sanders) told me that the day's lesson was pretty lengthy so she wouldn't have time to address my issue until after class. If I was to describe Mrs. Hayes I would say, picture a member of the "Cougar Club" (not the most active member by appearance but you knew she paid her dues). She was attractive for her age but not old enough to be aged. (She was far from being worn out.) She dressed like a housewife who still had office appointments. Her Ann Taylor/Banana Republic look was blemish free except for the chalk that would manage to work its way on to the back of her skirt. That's because she was one of the few teachers (or better yet females in the school) to have *top-shelf* (Top-shelf: n. when the upper area of the buttocks resembles the top of a bubble, it's not rare but not common either).

After writing the day's lesson, Mrs. Hayes always had a habit of standing too close to the chalkboard. Most of us guys didn't seem to mind; and what guy would mind chalked out top shelf? She was a school teacher by day but I bet after work, handcuffs and fishnet stockings replaced her briefcase. She probably had cocktails at a trendy spot called the "Teachers' Lounge".

So, I sat and waited. That class felt longer than an Alaskan winter. Receiving a bad grade on a test you thought was easy, was like showing up to a pizza party only to find empty boxes, and no sprite—total disappointment. A couple of classmates behind me asked, "How'd you make out?" To which I replied, "There seems to be some sort of mistake here. I know I didn't study much but there is no way in hell this is right. Half of these questions and answers were given in class."

It was there in my defensive rage that I realized that a single line on my Scantron sheet was left empty. Son of a bitch! That meant after that empty line, I put the answers in the wrong places. I immediately turned around to Keith who sat directly behind me and said, "Will you look at this shit!!! I skipped this answer by mistake and must have answered every question after that in the wrong column. I still passed while putting down wrong answers. What other proof do you need of my genius?" Keith reluctantly smirked as he looked back down at his own "C" paper. Keith and I often bragged to each other about test scores, so I didn't feel bad about rubbing it in his face this time.

After class, I presented my rebuttal to Mrs. Hayes and explained the unfortunate blunder. I told her that I knew something was wrong because over the last two weeks she had taught a remarkable lesson and that I had taken excellent notes under her example. With a straight-face look she said, "I'll let you retake the test later if you stop beating me in the head. Don't try to charm me. I am not one of your classmates." I gave her a straight-face look back and said, "I am not beating you in the head. It is a gentle tap, Mrs. Hayes."

She paused for a moment, smiled and while shaking her head with one hand placed on her chin she replied, "And just think, when I was filling up all my hot air balloons you were nowhere to be found." Mrs. Hayes was cool and I was able to take the test during the 5th-period lunch break. Crisis averted.

By the time I made it home that afternoon I remembered that I was expecting company. Actually, the aroma reminded me. I knew it didn't smell like eucalyptus and lemon grass just for me. Ivette! (Money Green/Black/Hospital White Chris Webbers). How could I have forgotten? I had met her a month earlier in the subway on my way to gymnastics class, which was more like stunt class. My cousin kind of got me started at an early age. We would work out, stretch and go over martial arts conditioning. From there, I found myself taking sidekicks to the abdomen and falling on queue. I was good at it but it just wasn't my passion. Every youthful soul loves flipping though, so the training and acrobatics remained in the weekend regimen. But, back to Ivette…

Ivette was like a Pepperidge Farm Milano cookie—half black. At 5'5 and about 131lbs, she resembled an hourglass with just a little bit more sand at the bottom of the hour. Her complexion, fair, just like that Milano cookie. She had olive green eyes with prism streaks of lighter green giving them a marble-like appearance. She put me in a jet setting mood. Cape Verde anyone? She stood with a self-assured posture either from discipline or confidence—chest out, shoulders back, neck straight, and head up. I liked it. I liked it like a daredevil likes a challenge. So, I put on my cape, ready for a bus jump.

I spotted Ivette as we exited the Manhattan-bound L train. She moved like she spent some time on a catwalk. She was about five yards in front of me. "Excuse me miss." She turned slightly. "One second. I know you from somewhere. One sec. I'm serious." She slows down enough for me to catch up. "I don't think we know each other," she replied like a boss talking to hired help. "If that was the best you could come up with, it was pretty corny."

"Of course it was corny, it was supposed to be. I just needed something to start the conversation with. We're talking now, so that corny line served its purpose."

From there we might have had three or four phone conversations. They were brief but always interesting. Whenever we reached a point in the dialogue where her interest was aroused, I would end the call claiming to have a priority that required my attention.

Ivette: "You mean to tell me if Halle Berry was in your bed completely naked and wanted you badly, you wouldn't try anything if you had a girlfriend?"
Me: "Completely butt naked? Nope!"
Ivette: "You're such a lie."
Me: "Well, umm...ok, it depends."
Ivette: "I knew it. Depends on what?"
Me: "Do I close my eyes when I kiss my girl?"
Ivette: "Wait. What? (She laughs with curiosity.) What does that have to do with anything?"
Me: "Oh snap, I just remembered I have to get a money order for my mother. I'll call you back later."

This kept her looking forward to the next encounter, something like dessert after a meal, but not *directly* after the meal. The chef will let you know when it's time. This meant that Thursday's special had to be orchestrated tastefully, so with my conductor's wand and chef's apron I commenced to arrange a masterpiece, attempting to edify the spirit and feed the soul.

She arrived ten minutes late wearing a polo-style shirt that was just long enough to be considered a skirt. By the way the fabric complemented her frame, I could tell it felt like jersey sheets. Everyone loves jersey sheets and I just so happened to have outfitted my bed with them that week (that was a casual conversation waiting to happen). A pair of ankle socks and tennis shoes (I think they were Stan Smiths) completed her ensemble. Yvette's hair hung a little past shoulder length and was styled with some volume with a reverse curl at the tips (sort of like an old picture of a young Vanessa Williams or that woman in *Weird Science*). I opened the door and led her in. "Would you like something to drink?" "Sure!" she said as she sat on the couch. The slanted angle of the sofa put her right in position to view pictures of various landscapes and people that were taped on the wall. I returned with two glasses of lemonade.

"Interesting, I like this one," she commented as she slowly sipped her lemonade and pointed to what I considered to be a spur of the moment good idea. The picture she pointed to was a shot of my reflection through a train car window while the train was in motion. Through me you could see the lights of the background buildings, as well as the words "FAT MIKE WAS HERE" etched in the train window. I wasn't expecting all that detail when I went to expose the film. "Yeah, I thought I was on to something when I slowed down the shutter speed for that shot. I figured as long as I stayed still, everything else would resemble the busy Apple", I told her. "It shows creativity. I could learn a lot about you just by looking at your pictures," she commented.

I thought to myself, of course she can. Why else would I sit you down in front of pictures? I needed Ivette to let that mind wander a bit before I return her to reality with some direction. Pictures serve as great middlemen for reference and interpretation of one's character. Onlookers are able to travel in time for a period that can only be told in retrospect and in response to her "I could learn a lot about you" comment. "Nice! You could have a future in the FBI or CIA, maybe even *Blue's Clues*." She laughed.

Actually, she laughed a little too hard because she accidentally broke wind at the same time. Flatulence is only a cool word when spoken, not in action and definitely not by someone I think could've been a centerfold. I truly understood the term 'Too much for your own good' or my good in this case. I was trying to make her comfortable and relaxed—but not that comfortable! On the bright side, it didn't smell and it wasn't done on purpose.

"Oh my god! I'm sooo sorry. That has never happened before. That's crazy. Oh my God, I am so embarrassed!" She repeated those lines over and over as if she was at a casting call auditioning for the role of the girl who just farted in my bedroom—fantastic work young lady, you got the part, you nailed it. I laughed along to ease the awkward tension. "Don't worry about it. Let's just say we officially broke wind, I mean the ice." Still embarrassed, she laughed with me while we both played it off.

Unfortunately for me, the damage was done. At that point, I was completely turned off. Maybe it would have been different if we had known each other longer. But she was new. There was no allegiance over here. I was sure my attraction could be reignited by another top model. I knew that after a hysterical outburst my friends would've said, "That's hilarious but get back in the game." No sir, I can't do it captain. I get turned off easily. Let's call this one a willing forfeit.

There was a reason I set the date up for Thursday and not Friday. Just in case something like that occurred, I could bail using a school-related excuse (well I didn't expect *that* to occur, but you get the point). Frankly, I thought I played it off well. After about 20 minutes of light conversation (jersey sheets included), I told her we should get out of the house and walk a bit. "I've been feeling like I was living in captivity all day."

Long story short, I navigated a one-way trip to freedom. The direction of our stroll led us right to her exit. "Wow! Isn't this the train you take? I guess because of time it doesn't make sense for us to go all the way back to my place, just to end up back here again." Ivette agreed. She told me it was fun and that we should do it again. "Call me!" she shouted as she walked down into the train station. "Will do," I echoed. We both knew if she held her breath on that one I would be getting a call from the authorities for being an accomplice to an assisted suicide. I chalked it up as one of those "Thursday duds". I went home, made a few calls and called it an early night.

Weeks went by and I still like Frosted Flakes because you don't have to add sugar. Oh, I forgot to mention that this was the period where I became a vigilante heartbreaker. It wasn't for any good reason either—boredom and the game had evolved. Let me explain. I had a few female friends in school that I conversed with daily. They were a tightly wound bunch of girls who often expressed their dislike with some of their peers (all potential targets).

The volume of these gripes would center on the presumption that someone projected a "holier than thou" attitude, which is totally their prerogative. But in the self-conscious, wolf pack mentality of high school, this persona could play against you. It's hard to convince the public that your shit doesn't stink when you all share the same bathroom. (Just for the record, that was an analogy, no one would be caught dead taking a shit in high school bathrooms, and by no one, I mean hardly anyone because somehow shit still showed up in those toilet bowls.)

Now for my part in this sensitive, microcosm of the real world. "Hey girl, let me at 'em. I got you. Who done it this time? Just point 'em out and I'll get to work."

The plan was simple and performed on numerous occasions. I would seek out the subject, acquaint myself, woo and then disassociate as hastily as possible. Sex wasn't the objective. A severed connection was. A smooth severed connection where people can't explain why the interest disappeared. Did I mention that high school can get boring? "Who is it?" I asked Robyn in between our classroom roll call. "You already know I'm not into cat fights," she replied. "Well it doesn't have to be beef. Anyone you find annoying or who just iggs you when you see 'em?" "Well, since you put it that way—Valerie is such a bitch and I don't really care for her. It's the second time this week that she spent the entire lunch break in the guidance counselor's office. She knows a bunch of other students are trying get their resumes done too. I wouldn't mind her getting caught up with something else."

She responded like there was a bigger reason for her dismay. Maybe Valerie did hog up all that resume time or was it was because Valerie caught the eye from Deshawn and Robyn liked Deshawn too. I knew this lioness had a thorn in her paw but explaining the real details of her choice wasn't my concern. My mother watched enough soaps at home, I didn't care for them at school. Venting while we paint fingernails wasn't in my descrip'. I just needed a target and Valerie was my bull's eye. She did slightly come off as a bitch though. She walked around like urban Miss Universe, with her head in space, arms trailing her waistline and the odd facial expression that made you wonder if her upper lip was searching for her nose.

I only remembered this story because my first encounter with Valerie (Silver 97' Airmax, all reflector) went nothing like planned. We had that cliché bump in the hallway. You know—the coed bump in movies where the guy and girl drop their books and all loose papers. Then both scramble to the ground to retrieve their disorganized possessions, only to touch hands in the process, which is followed by the first eye contact. Each character is dazed by the other. They stand together as if choreographed. Next, they exchange names with the briefest of pleasantries. After that, they walk away wanting to look back. And just when you think they won't look back, they do and catch each other. They smile. She sighs and then clutches her hands close to her heart making an upside-down "V" with her forearms. He smirks and his upside-down "V" is in the form of renewed confidence clearly visible from the perk in his step.

No sir! This particular incident wasn't so classic. Unlike the old days when students carried their books in belt straps, we wore book bags. There would be more than hand touching, and that mutual mishap would be the first impression that lasted.

The visual goes like this: Last semester we had an official bake sale; the sale proceeds would go to a local non-profit. Being the thoughtful guy that I am, I volunteered to bring in baked goods and assist in the sale process. There was also the added incentive from my Language Arts teacher who gave extra credit on the final exam for volunteer work. This participation involved sacrificing my lunch period to sell some gourmet delights.

Mrs. Meredith Stanlow, the organizer, happy with the sales outcome expressed her gratitude by giving us a sample of the product. "I'll have that last slice of blueberry pie and a piece of coconut custard, thank you." There was not much of a selection remaining. As it turned out, selling snacks at lunch time required little effort. I just called people out by their full government name.

"Yo! Yo! You hear me talking to you Marquise Anthony Roberts!!! I know you're coming right this way to get a cookie or brownie or something. It's only two dollars! What's two bills to a Baller? And not even two bills, but two bills? You spend more than that dry cleaning those Iceberg t-shirts."

It was true. What the hell was two dollars to fashion-driven, financially-uncultured kids who never learned the value of money because they never really worked for or earned the pair of two hundred dollar sneakers they begged their parents for? Which after two months, they had to go back to their parents and convince them they needed that same pair in black. The approach worked, especially with the fresh sneaker crowd.

This was the complete homemade bake experience - meaning Saran Wrap and no identifying labels. I'm carrying my dessert in a folded napkin. Equipped with my tasty delights I speed walked to my next class. Precision walking, I like to call it, and because the hallways are so crowded during the class change, precision at high speeds is essential. I was rushing because the homework the teacher gave out the day before was so easy that I didn't bother doing it. If I could get to class early enough I could do it there. Mr. Mitchell collected homework at the end of class. I think he was new to academia because it didn't occur to him that last minute procrastinators like myself would use his class time to complete any backed up assignments.

My English class was right around the corner and so was Valerie. She came around the bend and "Booyaka!!!" She ran right into me. She must have been rushing to her class as well. We collided like two individuals trying to move an unmovable force. To keep her from falling (and yes! I was walking that fast), I had to extend my arms to grab her. Between the initial collision and my heroic act, my sweet edibles were sandwiched between the top of my stomach and her bosom. "What the fuck?" we said simultaneously. We must have said it loud because I heard someone in the mass of students say "Jinx!!" I'm pretty sure it was Mark, happy with the opportunity for a late counter for me calling him out earlier.

For me the crash wasn't too bad. I had on a plain white tee. They look great fresh but are very inexpensive. (Just for clarity, not the 4xl baby dresses that came in style years later for tasteless adults & following teens. Mine fit like a futbol jersey.) Valerie, on the other hand. "Damn! I know this isn't funny but if you wore a blue shirt today no one would notice," I joked. She didn't see the humor. My napkin did little to stop the blueberry pie from assaulting her cashmere Ferragamo cardigan. "A good cleaners can get that out," I added.

My shirt wasn't that valuable so I intended to give it a one-way coach ticket straight to the garbage or maybe I would use it to dry freshly cleaned sneakers. "There's always Blue Man Group," I suggested. I know that last one was a little overboard, but I couldn't help myself. She knew it wasn't my fault. She wasn't even looking in my direction when we collided. Not that it helped the cashmere.

Valerie looked down at the fabric like she could see tiny fingers on the preserves, sure of their clingy nature. She had blueberry jam smeared on her shirt and sorrow and disgust smeared on her face. Making matters worse, I still had to rush to class. Though I would have loved to chat, flirt or even introduce myself, I couldn't. That homework wasn't going to do itself. "Umm, I'm sorry this happened, but I kinda have to go. Try soaking it." I had a bite of the custard before doing my homework. I still had that sweet taste in my mouth after class but I'm sure I left a bitter one in hers.

After that, Valerie and I became familiar strangers. Trying to make a move wasn't out of the question, it just seemed awkward, so I never pursued her. Our paths did cross again, actually in that very same spot. I was rushing for the very same reason but like two seasoned drivers, we had a better understanding of the turn. That whole first encounter was never the game plan but nonetheless, Robyn was able to work on her resume that day.

MEMOIRS OF A HIGH SCHOOL SNEAKER PIMP

Chapter 3

My bed feels like quick sand and my sheets like a blanket of grain. One fitted, one loose. The loose one is always harder to find, the fitted is always harder to maintain. My mind is smarter than my brain, my spirit is stronger than my physical shell, yet I insist on keeping the mold. For most, hindsight is 20/20 and foresight is cloudy. But what happens when fog turns to form? There must be another organ that can convey such dimensions or is your third eye truly alone, forced to never appreciate a visual stereo. I guess if I omit left and right there is no bias, there is no extreme, no contrast, only raw realism. How sad is one's death if that life had no beauty? Does a perfect flaw exist?

What do you say doc? Is it me? Am I losing sight? Is introspection a personal fabrication of the id or am I beyond myself, drifting even more to the boredom of being? If I imagine a mirror, how can my reflection be real? What do you say doc? I'm trying to inhale water in a world that only supplies air. I'm feeling the pressure to choose between what must be done and what I wish to happen. Isn't my want, semi-active passion waiting for Will to lead? Or do I do what must be done just to satisfy Destiny? She said it was my choice. What do you think?
He looks down upon me. Gray invades his hair like the new order of the

day. Rimless spectacles lowered to the bridge of the nose. Gravity's longitudinal lines distinguish him as experienced, so do the various plaques that adorn his wooden office walls. In a soothing tone, the doctor inquires, "What do *you* think?" "What do you mean, what do I think?" "I mean, what do you think? I'll take either one, Tiffany or Tamie. Remember, you're the one with the seasonal taste," Steph replied.

Damn it! Where did the doctor go? And why does my sofa feel like a therapists' couch. I must have fallen asleep waiting for Steph to decide which of my shirts he wanted to trade for his. We traded often when we both had items that the other wanted more. Day dreaming feels so counterproductive when I ask unanswered questions, especially when I feel an answer coming that might change the medicated way in which my glasses prescribe my views. There I go again. I don't even wear glasses.

He could have easily gone by the name Stephen (Stee-vin), but ever since he realized that the name "Steph" came along with a disguise-like sophistication—he favored the treatment, almost the same way some masculine men appreciate the misdirection that comes along with names like Jackie, Kelly, Pinky, Leslie, Kim, or even Stacy. He was tough, but the undertone of his name gave him a warm center or at least a perceived warm center. I was hip. Individuality is personal. Who was I to tell a hunter what outfit to wear in the field. We had planned a double onslaught.

Tiffany and Tamie were inseparable (Black/Red Air Bakin with the yellow laces and White/Navy/Yellow 98 Airmax). Let's call them Trinidad & Tobago for now. More like sisters without the bloodline, each one complimented the other. We admired Tiffany's curvaceous thick frame just as much as we loved Tamie's lengthy slender lines. We liked the style of Tiffany's braids—flat twists and foxtrot (yeah, I know foxtrot is a style of ballroom dance but that do should've had the same name because every girl with a two-step tried to pull it off) and in the same light, we dug Tamie's classic ponytail.

Steph and I decided to strike up a conversation with the girls during a school game. With the number two ranked high school basketball team playing their number one ranked rivals, it was sure to be an entertaining evening. Neither Steph, I nor the other team had any prior advantage with our counterparts. The fact that it was an away game alone made the trip worthwhile. A whole new group of girls would be there. The masses watch the high wire, cheered by excitement and hushed by the possibility of a wobble. It was like tight rope walking over a safety net filled with birthday gifts. Whether we made the connection we intended or not, we were liable to fall into something special. That is, if we fell/failed at all. It also helped that we loved everything basketball.

Just a background note: My high school was an academic fashion show. Occasions like this allowed the student body to replace the scholastic monkey with a Helmut Lang knapsack. This would give us time to fancy all the pretty colors, straps, zippers, patches, knits, silks, denims, micro cottons, suedes, cashmeres, leathers and the sure to be unveiled, never-before seen in a high school setting, someone's borrowed full-length fur. There was parental supervision but no parental guidance. All our superheroes were superficial. Our Joe Clark was absent for this event. You could now judge a book by its cover, even though the hardcover books often had paper covers attached. Don't get me wrong, I was just as stylish as the next guy, but that wouldn't be the first or last impression of me.

(Fun fact: Leather jackets were not allowed in my high school. The principle didn't want anyone getting robbed for their clothes after class let out. If you showed up wearing leather, you were sent home. That ban was enforced on school premises. For school events, not on school grounds, you can bet your ass that everyone was going to show out.)

Steph and I arrived eight minutes into the 1st quarter. The gymnasium was packed to the gills. Bright white lights reflected off of the bright wood floors, the canvasses of past victories hung from the ceiling. "WHOSE KIDS? OUR KIDS", our school motto inked on posters that served as a tapestry to this royal sport. Centered was the announcer's table and even though the scoreboard worked, the announcer's table had the original paper flip number system in effect. Eager eyes awaited that number flip when their team scored. The only thing missing here was the sound of someone yelling, "Gimme a beat!"

Oddly enough, the one thing that was not so classic about this high school pastime was the cheerleading presence. None of the most popular girls tried out or even wanted to be affiliated with cheering. Besides the cheerleaders themselves, no one cared or even paid attention to their performances. I bet if you asked most kids in my school how they felt about the cheerleaders, they would probably respond like, "Cheerleaders? Really! In this school? At what game?" (No offense to the cheerleaders, you ladies did a great job.) Team support was in abundance; it was just better recognized by students in the stands.

One bleacher stand was for friends and the other for foes—foes simply by the nature of rivalry. We spotted Tiffany and Tamie in the middle of teen spirit. Steph made the first move by shouting out at the referee as we walked the floor searching for seats. "Come on ref, just make one good call. I promise to get you the hat to match that shirt." Corey Parker went through two defenders by hitting them with the *Shammgod* then made a lay-up through what appeared to be an unchecked foul. Steph, not happy with the officiating, "Yo ref, does your wife work at Foot Locker or Lens

Crafters? Either way, your discount sucks!" I was laid back, cerebral funny. Steph was more open-mic night funny.

Our stand, mostly the lower level bleachers, reacted to his outburst with laughter, claps and foot stumps. I couldn't help laughing either, for three reasons: 1. That shit was hilarious, he said his wife works at Foot Locker! 2. Steph just introduced our arrival and 3. And most importantly, laughter makes you human—which makes a person approachable and the comfort that accompanies approachability slowly demystifies stigmas. I nudged Steph in the arm with my elbow to point out some open seats and told him to follow me. My direction would lead us right to Tiff and Tamie. Allison, a good friend of mine happened to be sitting right in front of T&T. ***The board is set up***.

A few more steps and, "Allison! I'm glad you're here. I've been meaning to talk to you. You know we're practically family and everything, but if we are going to continue to give each other the homework when one of us doesn't do it, I expect you to have the right answers. You know I don't check that shit before I hand it in. I trusted you. You got the teacher marking my paper with the, how could you get this wrong face and me looking at her like, 'Yeah, I wonder how I got that wrong,' I honestly don't remember doing that problem!" She giggled through her nasal cavity, seconds short of a full snort. "Stop lying, you know that didn't happen. I always double check my work," she playfully argues.

"Are you saving these seats for us?" I asked. "I guess so, looks like yall was about to take them anyway," Allison said with a smirk on her face. Ahh, the benefits of a female copilot but I'll get to that later. ***Pawns are disbursed***. Call it funny but Steph and I sat right in front of T&T even though there were seats directly beside them. "Why?" you might ask. Because when a person of interest has an opportunity to witness you interacting with other people, they see what you project and assume it's genuine—and for most people it is. The profile of your smile allows spectators to spectate. So, I put on a spectacle. It's the difference between watching someone unbeknownst to them and watching someone who knows they're being watched.

Let's just say I was smiling a lot. I wanted Tamie to infer as much about my character as possible. Steph goes along with the flow. He knows I'm up to something and team players ride it out. "THREE-POINTER BY NUMBER 21, COREY PARKER," the announcer yelled. "That's my boy," I said to Allison with the proud father look. I kept the conversation on the surface. If the idea is the core (me), you don't want your explorer (witness) getting lost in the crust of banter (I want her stuck on this generous smile not breaking down the content of the convo). ***The king surveys***.

A couple swooshes, a couple bricks and halftime was fast approaching. Allison was one of those girls that if you didn't tell her all your business, you might have actually tried to kick it with her. But that idea is counterproductive. It would be a little hard to tell the gazelle, that the lion in you is tame, especially when she gets exclusive testimony of your carnage.

There is always a girl that guys adopt as one of their own. Aside from her estrogen, she's like one of the boys, entitled to all the nuances of the pack. Hopefully, this sheep will be able to spot a wolf after being raised by them but most likely she won't and her skin will still be used as a coat for a wolf who sought out her warmth. Allison's refreshing character (Burgundy leather Clarks with the nutmeg brown soles) exceeded my desire to be with her physically. She was attractive but I liked her more for her personality. She was almost like a sister to the pack, but not quite. Actually, not quite at all but the love and respect was there.

"You want something from the snack table while I'm down there?" I asked. "Aren't you kind. I'll take a Reese's Peanut Butter Cup if they have it," she replied. As I made my way down the bleachers, my timing was perfect. T&T were both headed to the bathroom. So, picture this: my target is right behind me, we're headed in the same direction. All I have to do is turn around. This is probably the most opportune time to make a move. Who knows how this game will let out in the last quarter and I damn sure ain't chasing a girl across the court, hallway or avenue.

My thoughts were competing for the next move. It felt like I was playing myself, but I never want to play myself. With little time to think and the play in motion, I called an audible. Steph was in the bleachers flirting with Nestlé a few rows behind our seats. I signaled to him with the "It's on" look. I stopped and waved to Allison to accompany me. "What do you want if they don't have it?" I hollered from the floor. Okay, **knight just took bishop**.

The bathroom and makeshift concession stand were adjacent to each other. I could have gone there earlier and waited until they came out but something in my head reminded me that it's never that serious. By the time Allison and I made it to the hallway Steph was catching up behind us. Tiffany and Tamie were a few yards ahead. I'd already moved my rook two spaces. Next, I **revealed the queen**. I provoked an in-depth discussion with Allison, engaging to the curious ear and loud enough to invite an audience.

"Listen, I watch the way they treat their parents. Bottom line, if they're disrespectful to their own parents, oh boy, telltale signs. The same way your aunt or moms might've told you to pay attention to how guys treat their mother because if they respect and adore their moms, they will usually know how to treat you. It works the same for the other side. You're not the only person who notices. These are some standard rules. Everyone knows that. You can ask anybody." And by anybody I really mean, "Excuse me, Tiffany, can I ask you a quick question?" **Checkmate**! (Another form of *Space Invasion*)

Tiffany and Tamie both turned around with a slight look of bewilderment. We all knew of each other but the relationship was more casual than the topic. Wandering eyes in the hallway served as an appetizer for introduction. I deliberately sought out Tiffany's opinion and not Tamie's in this 'coming of age' discussion because that's what Tamie wouldn't have expected (even though, she was my real aim). If Tamie needed the answer to whether I was feeling her or not, my body language was the hint. Film students would have easily been able to interpret a snapshot of my stance.

Tamie and I had shared more encounters. We shared more classes. But I am more interested in her initial reaction when the first time I speak in her presence, it's not with her. I wanted our first interaction to provide information that wasn't given directly. Steph watched the setup, and like a double-dutch champ waited for the right moment to jump in. Any point he interjected with was done to keep the conversation flowing. Allison didn't realize how significant her presence was. She was a co-pilot on auto-pilot, holding one end of the rope while I did the turning. There was no work required on her part. I just needed her pheromones to act as the barbiturate. In an XY setting, introducing more X's relaxes the air. (Also not surprising, if you take that same equation and introduce more Ex's, the air gets f#@ked up really quickly.)

I wanted to explain this chromosomic phenomenon (yup, just made up a science term) about the x's and y's to Tamie when we met up a few days after the big game. I thought it could have been an interesting discussion. But that would have only helped if I liked my sirloin like a Sloppy Joe. I didn't peg her as a deep thinker but I could've been wrong. My choices: a conversation about female beauty and the subtleness of a wingwoman or Coach bags and the latest episode of *Moesha*.

If not inferred already, yes!!! That bait and snatch technique resulted in both of their numbers, in platonic fashion of course. The only way to get their numbers without being disrespectful to both was to show the same interest in both at the same time or show the same disinterest in both at the same time. That keeps everyone on an even playing field. They wouldn't object to my next move if they thought the game was on pause. Keep in mind that, if they were freaks, none of what I just said would matter (something I learned later in life).

When I later met up with Tamie, her pieces were incompatible with the board. We didn't really click. So, the game became checkers. Again, I kept it light but as usual became bored after a while. I made her dizzy for sport then eventually set my sights on Tiffany. In the process, I realized why some girls dislike girls. Loyalty is a bitch, and I was just trying to find her best friend.

If you are wondering about my partner in this play, Steph was just doing what wingmen do. He was offering that unspoken assistance. There is a special bond within a group, the feeling when others around you are married to the same goal. The prerequisite is not a membership of associates, affiliates, or even peers. Often camaraderie is simply the mutual recognition that we are the same. As far as Steph was concerned, camaraderie was always the sentiment of choice (simplified, he was a

Rider). The notion of "If it's not yours, it's for everyone" was well understood by the men of the cloth. We can all have their numbers, that part of the sport was free range. "You get a number, you get a number. And yes, you get a number," in my Oprah voice.

Only a personal cease and desist would void a written check (legit friends will never go after someone you claimed). This understanding made a friend's job easier because during those years, we tried hard as hell not to claim anyone. I also hooked Steph up with Nestlé a while back. She didn't think I knew because I still flirted like nothing changed. Silly rabbit, the Borg knows everything. Assimilation is unity (I just remixed some Trekkie slang). In regards to the game, Steph's last point came from my assist. "GREAT PASS BY NUMBER 32," I heard the announcer in my head. Friends like that didn't mind switching roles. '32' became a '23' when it was time to score. (From a Laker to a Bull.)

The non-academic world of high school moved fast. So did I. A month after the board was set up, I was sitting on Tiffany's bed looking at pictures of her and Tamie enclosed in heart shaped frames. "How'd you like that game?" Tiffany referred back to my last chess move. "That referee was a moron. That last foul should've been a flagrant. We would have won if not for that. On the bright side, my boy Parker did get a triple-double."

She didn't care about the game. It was a premeditated segue to discussing loyalty's best friend, which I hadn't entertained thus far. Interesting topic choice but I wasn't about to cock block myself if my answers didn't add up. Just so we are all on the same page here, a month later Tamie was a memory. She turned out to be a "Sloppy Joe" after all. So many marveled at her icing through the window but failed to open the bakery door. Texture changes the taste and I wasn't digging her frosting. It wasn't no buttercream. (If you caught that double negative, have a cookie.) Tiffany became the friend of choice. I really liked her too, just like tiramisu.

The current theme of formal dating didn't exist in my high school. Eloquent dinners, boat rides, and museum visits were excursions reserved for fully-grown adults on sitcoms and cinema. It took me two outings with Tiffany to realize that she would be a "Red Shirt". That means not yet on the team but a prospect whose potential might lead to induction. Coaches gave red shirts to athletes who exhibited potential. Minor discouragement wasn't uncommon when full access was denied but a "Red Shirt" was like going to a club and being on the guest list but not as a V.V.I.P. Most likely you'll get in, but you have to wait a bit.

Even as an adult, I was late joining the "dating" bandwagon and reluctant to succumb to the glazed, teary eyed, hand in hand, fingers interlocked walk into the sunset picture. I've seen a few guys take that route but that smooth sprinkle paved road was a plank, and that walk was a plunge. They drifted to sea and stared at the light of possibility so long that they forgot that in the middle of the ocean there is no visible land. The sun always sets on a wave. A ball and chain is now a weighted anchor. Go ahead, drown. I mean walk. Test the water. The only witnesses are a few birds who never cared but now acknowledge your existence and would love to witness your extinction. What a life. No point in diving head first if you only want your feet wet. Even speedboats have cruise control. Translation, we tried really hard to not claim anyone.

Nah man, high school outings were more often park meetings, nice strolls and house visits. Throw in a movie here and there for good measure. Hopefully, all are close enough to someone's house because if the rendezvous didn't start there, that's where you would've liked it to end up—in the land of seclusion. I usually preferred the girl's house. This way, I wouldn't have to worry about her lingering when it was time for her departure. It's ok to be blunt sometimes, but these sensitive operations call for peanut butter smooth. Chunky ruins a classic sandwich. It's always easier to leave on your own accord as opposed to the flip side—stuck waiting for this student mind reader to figure out what the "It's time to beat your feet" face looks like. She might have been absent on the day her etiquette class taught proper self-dismissal. So, if it could be avoided, I would always suggest that I do the traveling (that was that semester's motto).

To add to that, I liked to see people in their element, the comfort zone of slippers, ankle socks with the ball attached and the worn look that favorite sweatshirts and pants owe to affection. Honesty is an easier place to reach when these factors are present. The look should be, expecting company comfort, up-kept inviting, with the pretense of this is really "me." I also liked to travel outside of my own neighborhood. So, when the question of "my place or yours?" came up, it was an easy decision. Pardon me, sometimes when I verbally surf the wave is a tangent. I'm off my boogie board now.

The location is Tiff's place, of course. It was Sunday, a wind down day for most. Tiffany's parents were happily married but lived under different roofs, go figure. That plank diver had found a life preserver or maybe a scuba suit. Tiffany's mother was visiting her aunt this particular evening and her father usually didn't visit on wine down day. After our park stroll, it was the perfect time for a house visit.

Tiffany and I watched the idiot box for about an hour and then satisfied our hunger with Ray's thin crust pizza (it felt like 7 out 10 pizzerias were named Ray's) and Welch's grape soda. All the nourishment needed for the nutrient deprived adolescent. My slice was topped with chicken and tomato. Let's see—the dough for starch, tomato and tomato sauce for a double serving of vegetables (mom would have been proud) and the breaded chicken for protein—fortified bullshit. All your body needs when you are teen aged.

Our conversation was semi-interesting, only because it was translucent. Everything behind this pane glass was sexual. We played coy to our biological nature. "Is it me or is it hot in here?" I asked. She knew all too well the beginning to this one but it was really hot in her room so I was in the clear. I took off my shirt. I was wearing a smaller t-shirt underneath. I didn't ask her to disrobe in any fashion. Voice commands didn't have a receptive welcome at this point in the development (even if the voice in her head agreed with the request).

If you want something done you have to initiate, then play it by ear of course. Force was never my style, so like most guys I used pressure instead. Tiffany was in no way "easy". I had to exert more energy than I would have liked. It never went down. Her aunt's sister or that scuba diver actually did some constructive parenting. Something tells me I could have still broke her, but I respected her enough to save it for another day. My t-shirt didn't abandon me that time. That doesn't mean that ear kisses and light dry humping weren't in the picture. Arousal never left, he just watched the match from outside the ring.

Surprisingly, I left Tiffany's house that day feeling content with the situation. Maybe I was growing up. Maybe my morals appreciated hers. Maybe I wanted her to marinate with the idea of me so that when I bit her I could savor the taste. Who was I kidding, if allowed, would I have? Of course, I would have tried to make her scream my name in French—more like pronounce it with a French accent then say it in Spanish, Spanglish and then gibberish. I would have made her talk to me during and I would have laughed thinking that the only way I could describe it to my boys would be to tell them, "Imagine the sound of her trying to speak while sitting on a washing machine during the spin cycle." We all did it as kids with our house washers to hear the choppiness of our voices. Now picture her, take away the washing machine and leave the machine induced vocals. That'is the greatest memory never rode, I mean told.

I often thought I had a good and bad conscience that fought over the rights to my actions. I soon realized that they were friends all along who worked different shifts. My actions were based on who was on call. Girls like Tiffany were worth waiting for. Their grounded morals, along with their grounded personalities would carry them far in life. I could spot this awesome quality in young women at an early age and I respected it.

As far as my side in this daisy filled imagery of enlightenment, I still had wants and needs. So, in wanting to fulfill Tiffany's needs which involved the virtue of patience, I needed to fulfill my wants, which involved the virtue of *right now*. Teen wolf was the perfect gentleman as long as he could be an animal somewhere else. It was all about balance. Catch and release was a simple concept to abide by, when you had another bucket to take home. Though it may seem contradictory, this allowed me to be true to her and myself at the same time.

I saw myself like a company. And in that frame of thought, there was a position for her—always open and waiting. But since I am a company, productivity takes precedent over personal relationships. Positions are always open in different departments (where is an April when you need one). Lower-level management, upper-level management, the board of trustees, no position was untouchable within the company. That was because no one position made the company. Expansion and constant evolution was the theme. Let's simplify this idea and assume I'm a theater company, always casting for a star. Talent is what scouts live for. Scripts are character specific and every lead role has an understudy. You ever wore a fresh pair of rare kicks every day for a week? Of course you didn't. That's unheard of. Styling is based on options.

Chapter 4

"He's gonna jump!" someone screams. Startled by the commotion and curious about what was happening, I bust open the balcony doors to my terrace view apartment. Clumsily, I bang my toe on the barbecue grill while trying to move my rusted mountain bike out of the way. "Ouch! That hurts!" Hopping on one foot I am halted by the railing. It's the first time I'm glad the railing is there. I look down. People have gathered. Police barricades resemble Tetris pieces, the way they look just before you lose the game. The bigger the crowd gets, the more the pieces don't fit. Shouts of "He's really gonna do it this time," came from the other direction. I yell back into the chaos, "Who?! Where?! Where is he?!" Meanwhile, more voices are heard from the building across the street, "He's gonna do it! Someone, please stop him!"

Dammit! Where the hell is he? At this point I am one harness strap step away from falling over the railing. My insides are burning. I need to know. The mob is in a frenzy. I can't make out the Tetris pieces. A little boy wearing a lime green shirt with a reflective stripe across the chest, climbs on top one of the squad cars. Officers are too busy losing the tug of war for crowd control to notice him. His expression is visible from the evening's twilight. His face is serious, as serious as a six-year-old can look. He raises what appears to be a fingerless hand. He raises it as high as he possibly can. If that limb was the arrow on a compass, it must have been facing north. From what seemed to be a thousand feet away, I can finally make out his fingers. The point of that digit, having never experienced a rough surface, held a sturdy form and clear direction. I stare so intensely that my eyes begin to cross. My stomach has turned into knots. He's pointing directly at me. In my moment of consciousness, the yells stop.

Every individual face in the mob, in the building across the street, is looking at me. My eyes feel like telescopes. I can make out every cheek, every frown, the cornea, pupil, and iris on every face. Those eyes turn bloodshot. Those blank expressionless faces mask a horror that can't be felt in the now, only anticipated in the moments ahead. In the most horrific display of synchronization, those faces fixate on me.

I am frozen stiff for what seemed to be five minutes but was really two short seconds, according to the skinny hand on the large clock in the supermarket window. My entire body has distanced itself from my nervous system. The only reason I know I still have a body is because I can see it. I feel nothing though. My clothes sway and dance in the breeze. My soul is locked in a body that it has no control over. I feel like I'm trapped in a shell. Surprisingly, I still feel the pain in my toe caused by that barbecue grill.

Moments pass. It's slowly coming back to me now. The tingling sensation that you feel when trying to wake a sleeping limb is happening. Each vein, each artery playing their part in the give and go. The breeze is cold. I can feel its temperature through the seams of my pants. My foot is in agony. My fists are clenched in preparation. My eyes are steady and focused—so focused that I could burn a hole through a hole. My vision has no placement and I am left looking at what's not there. I can't stand here anymore. My body won't allow it. My mind hasn't agreed yet but reflex overrules thought. I will not wait for what awaits me. My muscles tense up, contracting with pain. I jump....

Clearing the railing as if I had a running start. Formless in my dismount, I'm falling up. The ground isn't getting any closer. It's shrinking. Its substance marginalized by the bigger picture. Sucked up like in a vacuum from my balcony in the open space. I display all the characteristics of falling. My arms and legs are flailing. Homeostasis and equilibrium are off trying to find my body's coordinates. Things are becoming smaller. Usually things get clearer as you make your way to the end but for me things are becoming cloudy in the beginning. I travel in regression. I only see what's in front of me as I'm being pulled from behind, falling up.

Past the clouds, past all three layers of atmosphere, floating in space. Still being sucked back, just at a lower rate of speed, I am going somewhere. I am slowly falling into place. My back gently bottoms out as I fall up into my bed, unmade as if awaiting my return. I'm finally still. The mob, the boy and *Tetris* are vaguely remembered as I reflect on the journey. My sheets decide to cover me. I am being tucked in from head to bruised toe. I close my eyes. I open my eyes. I am calm.

A slice of sunlight pierces through my blinds to invite the day. Birds are attempting to sing. Squirrels are heard rustling through the leaves in my front yard. I never got around to cleaning those leaves. I've been procrastinating for almost a week. If my mother could hear the noise these animals were making, she would flip. Thankfully, her room was located in the back of the house. The squirrels sound like little four year olds running in a playpen full of shredded newspaper. Shouldn't they be on a telephone pole practicing their trapeze acts? Now it sounds like a group of squirrels found the squirrel that stole their nuts and a little squirrel ass whipping is taking place. I thought to myself, "If they are still out there when I leave the house, I'm going to have fun scaring and chasing those squirrels around the yard." About ten minutes passed before I started to make my way outside. They were grouped together in the corner. I thought about jumping in that corner and yelling, "Boo!" Then I remembered that we live in the big city. These squirrels probably have big balls, a Napoleon Complex and a small posse.

"I don't want any problems Mr. Cheeks. I would greatly appreciate if you and your fuzzy buddies would get from round these parts." Mr. Cheeks mulls it over in his head, looks down at the dried-up leaves, looks at me, looks at his furry-tailed desperados, then snaps his tiny razor-sharp fingers. They humbly walk out of the yard like civilized train rats. But just as the last miniature goon exits the front gate, he turns around right in front of a pile of leaves, kicks them at me, flips me the bird and says, "Wake the fuck up."

I usually had multiple dreams but none that connected so seamlessly. The more I moved around in my seat, the more the first dream faded into a filing cabinet that I hadn't yet learned how to access. My class, along with every other sophomore class, was in the auditorium. We were all called to a mandatory assembly. This meeting excused our scheduled class attendance. My history test was detoured and the next day was a holiday. For the most part, I and every other student didn't care what holidays were coming up. As soon as the words "No School" followed, we honored that day like side chicks honor quality time.

That break gave me two more nights to study for my history test (even with the added cushion, I would still procrastinate until the last minute). Effective procrastination—some kids get it, some don't and most try and end up with grades that reflect their unfamiliarity with this lost art. That mandatory second period assembly was the official kick off of our Annual AIDS Awareness Day, commonly referred to by some students as "No Sex for a Week" day. That day was more than just the faculty's attempt to fill in the missing gap of personal parenting with mass-produced campaigns of celibacy and sexual responsibility (which were good campaigns I might add). It was a wake-up call. Some of these chicks and dudes were burning (Yikes!).

Luckily, I was able to avoid that experience. I did hear stories though. Plus, I am visual person, so I could see it. And if I could see it then I could feel it (in my mind). I was traumatized just thinking about it. I was unscathed due to good judgment. I would like to thank myself first, and then my brothers for showing me what the dirty part of a flower looked like (and a boardroom meeting handshake goes out to you fellas). This day served as a public service announcement for S.T.D.'s in general.

This annual show and tell had three parts. The first, which was the part I slept through, entailed Mr. McKinley, the Dean of Students, going over what he called "Housekeeping Details." Grades…blah blah blah…attendance…blah blah blah…your future…blah…family values…blah…contribution to society. Mr. McKinley rambled on for about 15 long minutes until the guest speaker arrived. "Please folks, act like you have some home training and give St. Magdalene's Clinic a round of applause for taking time from their busy schedule to be here today."

"Thank you, ladies and gentlemen, for having us here with you. My name is Dr. Walter Cox, but during our Q and A panel later this afternoon, you can refer to me the same way my friends do, as Dr. Cox. I am here representing St. Magdalene's Medical Clinic. On your way out, there will be volunteers passing out condoms and literature." Someone yelled, "I hope not the lambskin ones, I might be allergic."

Immediately the students were tickled. Even the reserved students laughed. The only odd balls were the teachers, who stood straight and nodded in zombie-like fashion to Dr. Cock-a-doodles contraceptive generosity. "You got those in extra, extra-large? Those are the only ones I use doc!" someone shouted from the back of the auditorium. "Literature! Does this mean I have to read to her first before we can get it poppin?" another outburst came from the left. Only a ringmaster would have been able to control this crowd.

The good doctor respectively paused while the momentum of the laughter slowed to a halt. "We who work at St. Magdalene's Medical Clinic don't promote sex. We promote safe sex, if that's the choice you guys decide to make. I personally recommend hitting the books." The zombies were now the students who looked motionless in response to his humor. The teachers were the only ones nodding in confirmation of his message. They still managed to look like odd balls though. The good doctor then addressed my peers and me, with a smirk, as if knowingly about to drop the ball. "For every student in this room who has had sexual intercourse, do me a favor and raise your hands. Don't worry, it won't be for long, a little participation, please people."

Slowly but surely, most of us guys raised our hands. Some guys raised two. For any guy who was a virgin, that wasn't the ideal time to let your classmates know. A few bold ladies threw up a finger. Marlin, the class clown, slouched low in his seat and raised two hands and a foot. Again, the wild crowd was amused. "Ok people, I need you guys on the left to lower your hands...Ok, now you guys on the right, lower your hands. Ok, people in this middle section here. I need every row that is behind...umm...Mrs. Hayes, to lower your hands." Surprisingly enough, organized participation from this A.D.D. student body was working. Mrs. Hayes was standing in the left aisle right outside of the middle section. Dr. Cox paused before delivering his punchline "Now for the people in the front who still have their hands raised, one out of every two of you has a sexually transmitted disease. The statistics are real, folks."

Everyone quickly lowered their hands in disbelief. The roar of shock rose over the volume of the guest speaker's microphone. After that announcement, everyone was wide awake, grossed out and eager to hear the latest stats. The numbers sounded like high scores for a failing grade. Any percentage was a bad percentage when you were part of the affected population. Fifteen minutes passed and we had heard every good reason not to be sexually active. But no, my friends, it wasn't over yet.

There was still a finale we were accustomed to before "Doomsday" was complete, but in the meantime, we were redirected by comic relief. A few of my classmates had volunteered to perform a dramatization of teen pregnancy, teen peer pressure, and every negative aspect of teen sexuality and promiscuity. This was no performing arts school by any stretch of the imagination. The acting was on par with a low budget porn mixed with a telenovela.

The whole dramatization was funnier than any other comedic display that day. Did I mention atrocious acting? "Hey Emily, you know I love you. Can we do it now?" Then there were the delayed line cues. "What? Oh! Timmy, do you have protection?" "Ah shucks! I don't, but don't worry. Even though I've never been tested before and I've had a few partners, I don't have diseases. Trust me, I would know if I did."

After about 30 minutes of *When Acting Goes Wrong*, it was time. We had finally reached the point where stomachs turned, throats gagged and eyes watered. The lights dimmed, the projection screen lowered, and the slide show began. Those next few minutes would be embedded into the developing psyches of every person who was or ever thought about being active. This was why we students fasted from the mere thought of our sexual desires. The stats were very scary, especially since they said the infected were learning among us. But that still wasn't enough to reform us sinners from our lustful ways.

Seeing was believing (this was pre-David Blaine and Chris Angel spectacles). Why Emily, why! Why did you trust him? Look how dirty his sneakers were. Dr. Cox pulled out a laser pointer from the outside pocket of his lab coat to assist in the repulsion. The first clip appeared on screen. "What is that? What the hell is that?!" yelled a perplexed Steph from the center of the auditorium. "That's just not right. No sex for me. I'm abstinent. I'm gonna practice abstinence," Tony cried from somewhere in the back.

I thought my ears where playing tricks on me. I could have sworn I just heard a girl say, "My cousin had that!" "Don't act like you've never seen vegetables before!" Marlin yelled out. It was horrific and more frightening than *A Nightmare on Elm Street*, *Jason*, *Poltergeist*, *Night of the Living Dead*, *The Exorcist*, and *Alien* (the first one) combined.

Every clip was somewhat recognizable as genitals and what looked like some sort of medley of sautéed vegetables. There was a deformity, a growth, a block party of diseases parading their independence, only to leave the streets covered with trampled hooligans and the visual of an on-strike sanitation force. For heaven's sake, where was the clean up? Some pictures looked like sun dried potato salad topped with fermented yogurt mold.

Ok, that's it for my description of being *Scared Straight*. We could've made a joke out of anything, and we always did. But rhe consequences of our passion-driven actions was clear. There were plenty of things to laugh about in terms of what we said and what we saw, but nothing was funny about how we really felt. A dose of reality can have that effect on the youth.

A week went by and eventually the jokes subsided. The memories partly faded. We went through a stage where we mourned our libidos. We wept for our impotence and buried our testosterone. But like the happy ending of a fairytale, we were resurrected with the promise of better days, adjusting our crotches and correcting our pants. This was high school; a week was long enough. That's like a lifetime or so in adult years.

The same dark-suited, reaper-like messenger in my head who called a stop to production—blessed with the consent of the highest court in the land and sanctioned by the king—had reentered the chamber wearing a pair of khaki shorts, a graphic tee and a pair of Jordan XI's with the crystal clear soles (the ones he wore in the game, not the re-retro's that came back out every three to four years with slightly different materials because the original factory was supplied by a slightly different sweatshop). He pulled a folded note from his back pocket, unfolded it and read aloud in a projected voice directed at the arena. "Let the games begin!!!"

Things were finally back to normal and just in time too. There was a new girl on the horizon. I had charted out her course. I was on a steady pace. I cut off my engines. The breeze was in my favor. She would've gotten wind of me soon. I left the battleship behind; things tend to get messy when you try to swat a fly with a waffle iron. Thought I'd go commando, single occupancy craft. Did I forget to mention that I love women? Remember love is synonymous with understanding. I love them for what they are, for who they are, essential to the matter of my being. Let me slow that down a bit. I wasn't talking procreation yet. I still had S.A.T.'s to take.

Crystal (Pepsi Blue/Black Max Penny's) wasn't new to my radar. She wasn't even new to the school. She was just new to my agenda. Crystal was 5'8 and about 140 pounds. Thickumms I say! She had butterscotch skin, a feather soft hairline and a refined presence. Princess-like if you asked me. She had soft apple cheeks (I'm still referring to her face) and full lips (let me pause to applaud those lips, the top and the bottom). I was pretty sure she knew who I was. Girls in my school always thought they were helping out the coop by briefing the new chick. Sorry ladies! That didn't always help. I just made grill promotion at KFC and that chicken was born to be eaten. I just needed to find out what was going into the bag: honey mustard or barbeque sauce?

It wasn't that I was detached from my emotions. I just hadn't let them leech off of the young flesh of my masculinity. I knew things would change. I figured in my sixties I probably wouldn't care for selvedge denim. By that time, I would have been wooed by the feel of imported fabrics that only slacks and dress pants can deliver. I also felt that ten years from then I could be the most compassionate cuddler a woman has ever felt, but at that point, spooning was impossible with my fork-ing attitude. If this ugly duckling was destined to be a swan, I really wanted to enjoy being ugly first, before it was time to change the color of my coat.

Crystal and I were assigned to the same group in my computer programming class. I probably would have pursued her eventually, but this opportunity was like tossing chum in the sharks' pool. My fin was bound to show up. The intro was short. Group requirements forced us to exchange home numbers. Patience was the only virtue, timing, the only craft.

We were supposed to have weekly group meetings to discuss our progress. Not I captain. That was out of the question for me! I told my group mates we'd just touch base over the phone and if it got too hectic we could jump on a conference call. I had to call three group members for progress reports weekly. Crystal's call was always saved for last. She had the sweetest voice, polite yet assertive. I called her the week after that *Doomsday* presentation.

Me: "The best part of that class is hearing the end of the period bell. Don't you hate MS DOS? No one even uses that crap. Have you seen the screen? That shit is black and green. Looks like a computer from *Trading Places*."
Crystal: "Trading Places?"
Me: "Yeah, with Eddie Murphy. You Know, Lookin' good, Billy Ray!!!"
Crystal: "Billy who?"
Me: "You never saw? We are going to have to get you updated on the classics. After this project, I think we need a movie night."

She could hear the smile in my voice. She could tell I was casually flirting over the phone. I can't recall a teenage conversation that didn't involve flirting. I flirted with girls I liked. I flirted with girls I didn't like. I even flirted with my female teachers. I couldn't help it. It was like a Pitbull puppy tearing up an old sock just for tearing's sake. He can't be pacified with a teething ring. I like to look at it as practice for something more to come. And like that cute puppy, any sock, shoe or boot will do. The programming assignment was fairly easy, a page of commands here and a page of executions there. We finished ahead of time.

*(Before I continue, keep in mind that **I am not Will Smith and this is not the movie Hitch**. I am only noting my observations and actions. No manual can show you how to be yourself.)*

Crystal was definitely a princess and I knew which one. That made all the difference in my approach. There were two types for me; One princess was well aware of her lineage. Her tiara worn proudly on her head. She would never be caught without it, at least not outside the courtyard. Her visible cloak was garnished with the kingdom's royal crest. Her sleeve did not bare her heart. The cuff of her silk crochet blouse was embroidered with her majesty's (her mother's) expectations and rules. (Rules are made for order and sometimes just made for the people who will follow them.) This princess relished in her family name and expected slightly more than she had earned. Her royalty was her everything. Not to discredit her warm center, she was still approachable but you had to break through several layers of posh and ego first.

The other one, Crystal's type, was instantly lovable—kind and naturally docile until provoked. Her coat was transparent; you didn't need to break the shell to figure this out. Sherlock Holmes never opened his briefcase. I knew this well because we had met before, not Crystal per se. It was a different person, same personality. She expected to be treated the way she would treat you. A fair maiden, everyone in the forest loved her. She might have been an easy target for most, if not for the queen's tentative schooling.

Instead of movie night, I invited Crystal to a L.I.V.E.WIRE (LiveWire) concert. At that time L.I.V.E.WIRE, Crise P and Theophilous London were on tour in the states. My cousin Rona worked for a booking agency and whenever Live was in town she would bring me tickets. And once in a blue moon she would dish out some backstage passes. Rona tried to give me what she didn't have as a teenager—a cool older cousin. This just so happened to be that blue moon. When I told Crystal that we were going to meet L.I.V.E.WIRE in person after the concert, she almost collapsed. Now I'm not into groupies, especially if they're not mine, however L.I.V.E.WIRE was my favorite artist, so I gave her a pass.

We met in front of Madison Square Garden. Crystal was wearing pointy toe yellow suede boots with a chrome pencil thin heel, a pair of black tights that outlined her 'legs for days' frame, and a thin knit Coogi sweater dress that appeared to be the exact same match to the heels. At the time, that particular knit was a newer model and had faces cleverly woven in the fabric. "Who is your stylist? Please give them a raise. You look incredible," I greeted her. "Oh stop," she replied. Elegant in her stride, with a switch that could strike a match if one was close enough. "You look like candy." Flattery was the best form of flattery.

The performance was high energy from start to finish. Live's saying "It's your Favorite" were exactly the words I wanted stuck in Crystal's head when she thought of me. Rona had told Live about her little cousin. So, when the show was over we were all invited onto Live's tour bus. Of course I kept my cool. I'm my own biggest fan, but he was so down to earth I thought I was kicking it with one of the homies. We chillaxed in his mobile mansion for about twenty minutes before parting ways.

Before Crystal and I made it across the street, Live opened the bus door and yelled to Crystal, "Yo girlie, you got yourself a good dude right there." Immediately I thought to myself, "I love you Rona, and draws, draws, draws, panties, panties, panties." The opposite of a monkey wrench is a high five. That's that camaraderie I was referring too. Live's assist put my mind on fast forward; already anticipating the next quarter. I wondered if Crystal wore matching sets and if she didn't, I wondered if the colors were in the same family like pastels, neons or earth tones. I wondered if she shaved a landing strip or kept it clean cut. There was no pressure though. If I was Peter Parker about to do my spydee one-two, Rona and L.I.V.E.WIRE just threw me the Venom suit—and we all know what venom does to the body (instant edge). I relished the idea of the inevitable.

Crystal and I were intimate three times in my head before we ever had sex. And yes, when the time did come, the sex was way better than all three mental intimacies. Unfortunately, with the exception of April who had been cut from the team, I was never intimate with the same girl more than once. (I know I made an exception for official slides, but even fun times had their maturity date.) That's probably why I did it like it was my last time, because it actually was—with her.

I want to say that I wasn't doing it on purpose, but I did notice a pattern. Mind you, most were not one-night stands, in the "Hit it and Quit it" sense. I kept in touch and made sure to never make empty promises. I put in real work for the situations that required it, but again, those soda pop ventures would flatten out; The Fizzle effect. That forbidden forest where the princess lived would become a hidden forest that had lost its place on my map. I knew she was there but I wasn't moved to visit. Her image would be framed with the other princesses. The "Hit it and Quit it" saying needed to be adjusted. I never quit. I slowly waltzed off stage. The audience could still see me moving from the mezzanine. They just wouldn't know if the show was over or if intermission was looming. Most of my relationships ended with commas.

(**Fun fact**: Sad, selfish but true then and still applies now in many cases. More often than not, many young women were pleasured sexually by young men, by way of ego and not that young man's genuine desire to please them. A guy had to make sure that if the relationship or connection-ship ended badly, he didn't have to worry about someone bad mouthing his pipe game. It actually worked in his favor if he excelled in that department, because if she did tell her friends, it became free advertising. **Double fun fact**: The really smart girls knew the flip side of publicity and kept the stories to themselves. How many times can you tell someone about a good movie and expect them not to want to see it.)

Chapter 5

Shhh!!! There is an alligator in my room. He's sitting on my couch. He's not looking at me but I can tell he knows I'm here. I slowly untangle the covers from my leg and pull them off. I have a little baseball bat beside the box spring of my mattress. My mother's good friend gave it to me after I helped her move into her new apartment. Looks like it could be useful during a road rage incident. I try to reach for it, but the bat sinks into my wood floor as if laid on cornmeal dense quicksand. "Fuck" I say under my breath. I didn't know wood could do that.

I've been collecting knives since I was five years old when my father's friend gave me my first dagger. I used to carry it in my white Fruit of the Looms. In hindsight that small knife reminds me of a caveman's first nail file. He whispered in my ear and said, "I'm giving you this because I know you are responsible. Don't tell your mother." My everyday carry knife should be in the belt loop of my pants. I was pretty tired when I went to bed last night, so my clothes should still be on the floor in the same spot where I flung them. I slid off the mattress—the side furthest away from the alligator. Then I dragged my dungarees by the cuff toward me, slow enough not to disturb my company. My knife wasn't there! What was I thinking anyway? I never heard of someone killing a pocket knife with an alligator, I mean an alligator with a pocket knife.

The alligator shifts his position, not facing me yet but I know that's bound to happen. Maybe I can take my sheet and wrap it around his face. That should buy me some time. I grab for my fitted sheet because the elastic might make the job easier but in an instant that sheet is no more and I am left with a handful of sand. The alligator turns around, attracted to the sound of the falling grains. He must have been about 20 feet long and weighed a few tons. I don't understand how those measurements made it into my room.

He stares at me. His eyes pierce through mine. I am barefoot and only covered by my boxers. He's not moving. I'm not moving. I'm not frozen. I'm just thinking about the outcome of my next move. He watches me think and he probably doesn't like the foundation of my thoughts. His vertical lid cleans his eye. Step by calculated step he clears way from the couch. Water and moss suddenly ruin the floor. Vines and leaves begin to enchant the walls. My ceiling fan grows a beak and flies away.

This has to be the first time I've seen an alligator grin. He is massive in size. The scales of his skin look like bathroom tiles and his arms and legs like locomotive parts. He stands totally frozen. I am watching him think and I do not like the foundation of his thoughts. I hunch over to a crouched position. The handle of that nail file pinches my obliques. It's like I am a little boy all over again.

The past catches up to now. I am back in my white Fruit of the Looms. He launches at me with his mouth open so wide that he would have knocked down the ceiling fan if it hadn't flown away. I charged straight ahead, dagger in hand. The calm water between us is disturbed. Just as he goes for the bite that compels his jaws to sever the air, I dive inside the dark cave that is his mouth and land in my bed.

That was definitely a weird dream I had. It felt like I was trapped in the book *Wild Things* or *Jumanji,* but no one came to my aid. I was forced to make those tough decisions by my lonesome. I dozed off in the back of a cab; a tan Lincoln Town car. My older brother (nine years my senior) and I were on our way to his girl's house. Well not his girl but a girl that most likely wanted to be his girl (that's how little brothers think). Let's call her Dawn. The conversation they had the day he received her number involved family. Naturally, I was plugged in to meet Dawn's younger cousin, Amanda. There was no need to ask my older brother about Amanda's physical appearance, he knew my style. He would have already conveyed my expectations.

This was his first time meeting Dawn since their initial number exchange. Dawn lived in the neighborhood. The cab ride took about six minutes. We entered an apartment building across the street from my school. I wondered if I knew Amanda because I passed that place every day and if I did, how funny this would be. There was no need to ring the bell, a tenant was coming out. "Don't worry ma'am, I'll hold the door for you." We walked past the front desk where my brother signed in as "Flash Gordon" in the visitors' log-in book. We made our way through a small atrium to the elevator.

The elevator was fragrant, not because maintenance did an exceptional job cleaning, but as we walked in, the guy who was leaving the elevator smelled like his clothes were dipped in cologne. He probably had a monthly budget for smell goods. He wore an oversized set of headphones with music blasting. My brother and I could hear every word to Mary J.

Blige's "I'm Goin' Down", anticipation for a hot date, perhaps. His odd bounce to the music suggested a lack of mastery of his body's mechanics. In layman's terms, he was a doofus.

When the elevator doors closed, my brother and I chuckled at the same observation. We went up to the third floor, through the corridor, down the hallway, made a left, a right and another right. My brother dusted the bottom of his white, purple and blue Huaraches and me my white and green Gel Lytes as we stood above the "Welcome Home" doormat. A heavy knock and Dawn (C.F.M. Pumps; ladies, you know what I'm talking about) answered. Though the building was old, Dawn's place had a modern style feel; with eggshell white walls and flat white ceilings. A computer desk, big projection screen TV, burgundy leather loveseat and matching sofa with chaise furnished the space. The living room and kitchen were conjoined in the center of this pre-war apartment, with bedrooms located at each end of a short hallway.

"Yeah, she'll like him," Dawn said to my brother. "I told you he looks like a smaller version of me. Where's my hug?" my brother asked. He picked her up in the air with ease, with a bear hug just shy of crushing. She liked it, and I made a mental note. "Amanda! Your guest is here!" Dawn sort of shouted from the doorway.

Amanda (Michigan Navy/Varsity Maize Dunks) opened her room door and walked out in a pair of beige Bally's, designer jeans (Soho designer, not anything from the mall) and a canary yellow blouse only a pirate's daughter would wear. She was caramel glazed, high maintenance in a T-Boz body—I could dig it. "Nice to finally meet you. My cuz told me about you." She extended her hand in my direction. I took her hand and lightly pulled her in closer. With our hands at each other's waistlines I leaned in and kissed her cheek. "It's a pleasure." My brother looked at

Dawn and said, "My work here is done," then he grabbed her by the waist and pushed her in whatever direction he assumed her bedroom was in. I imagined their phone convo was pretty interesting because they both seemed too comfortable for a first visit. We followed their lead as Amanda invited me into her room.

In Amanda's room—not a cocaine conversation but a gateway drug, nonetheless.

Amanda: "Sixteen? You just turned sixteen this year? You're a baby. I'll be robbing the cradle." (She sung-spoke her statements like the melodic tone of some Caribbean dialect)

Me: "Yeah, I just turned sixteen this year. I will agree with you, in most cases, age does represent one's experience and if not of a certain age, the lack thereof. But here, it's just a number. You weren't thinking about age when we met in the doorway. You weren't thinking about age for the last five minutes of light chitchat. Ok, I threw you a number, a number you weren't expecting. And now, after reading the pages of what could be the best literature that has ever invaded your book club—now you want to judge by the cover? How does that work when you already like my story? Are you willing to give up a future memory? Realistically, you should bite the cookie before you get the fortune. And if you do take the fortune without eating the cookie then you just missed the experience of the cookie. I'm sure you have a sweet tooth."

Amanda: "Hahaha!!! Did your brother tell you to say that? Ok, Mr. Philosophy. You are interesting, very interesting. I'll give you that, but I still feel funny about this. Do you know how old I am?"

Me: "Uhhh…ummm"

Amanda: "I'm twenty-three years old. When I was seven, you were in the race of your life, your first swim meet. Really! When I was eight years old, and my dad bought my third bicycle, you were falling on your ass looking for balance. When I was nine, changing my little sister's diaper, you were still pissing yours. When I had my sweet sixteen party and my girlfriend Cynthia couldn't make it, she was probably babysitting YOU!" (She laughs during and at the end of each statement.)

Me: "You think that's funny? It's not going to be funny when you're the first person on the bingo line. It won't be funny when your breasts lose their self-esteem, when your dentures look like Halloween props, when your knees and lower back ache just because you decided to wake up, when one whisker grows off that beautiful face of yours and one of your eleven cats decides to play with it while you're sleeping. And when you fall, you know the one when I was discovering balance, that same fall can paralyze you."

Her: "That is so extra. I'm not that much older then you"

She appreciated the wit. Our conversation finally got past the age interrogation. You can't be held in detention for slipping someone a Mickey if you explain to them what a Mickey is (I do sympathize though. If this was real court, Statutory and Mickey would not get along). Amanda realized that I was mature for my age or any other age for that matter. She had fun talking with me. She said I made her laugh a lot. And for me, it was exciting, an extra dose of serotonin running through my brain. Our dialogue had a different feel. She had to be the most seasoned girl I'd encountered thus far; more seasoned than my usual dodgeball contestants.

No curfews. No rules, just two independent souls. Well! One soul still lived with his mom but that would change soon. Once 18 years of age, this bird was leaping out of the nest whether his wings worked or not. Amanda and I had chemistry. We got along well. I found myself being attracted to her other qualities and not just her womanly adornments, though I still admired her adornments.

After about a week of lengthy phone babble, this "Teen Wolf" grew a mustache. I threw the word "sex" in every conversation we had like a punctuation in a phrase. She wasn't new to this. She probably had an on-again off-again college boyfriend who was now in the off season. She probably didn't, but that was the hot summer forecast that deterred me from wearing those warm stuffy feelings that are still neatly folded in my drawer. The bottom line was, I wasn't completely sure if she wanted me. I had a hunch, though, and I hold my hunches in high regard. I often shared adolescent stories like this with my mother, only the PG-13 ones, of course. I told her about Amanda.

My mother: "Twenty-three?! What the heck does a twenty-three-year-old woman have in common with a sixteen-year-old boy?" I arched my right eyebrow and stood straight with my shoulders back. "Ok, sixteen-year-old young man."

So pleasant in making her case, she smirked at me the whole time. My mother knew I was going to be sarcastic and over-the-top in my response. She knew it well and got a kick out of it.

Me: "Listen lady, all of this glory cannot just be for teenage girls. I can't deny someone a cup when trying to drink from the fountain of youth and yes, young, but a young man. You know I can probably pull some of your friends, too! But you see, my wisdom tells me that friendship is important and I do not care for any part in the degradation of your good relationships. But, if you try me woman, I'll have one of your girlfriends calling you asking to speak to me. And you will know something is up when you realize they don't have any children your son's age. I am man, hear me roar. The alpha and the Omega will be the watch your girlfriend buys me in her attempt to persuade me to make time for her."

When I was done with my rave, my mother and I both laughed hysterically. Even funnier was the fact that after my podium speeches I had to take off my shirt and flex in front of her. "You see these muscle cubes woman? Your lady friends want a piece of this. I think I will start taking bids," still on my campaign. "You are too much," my mother replied. "To the victor goes the spoils!" I yelled aloud. What made these episodes even more sitcom-funny was that if my older brother, Ta, saw me flexing and talking smack to my mother, he would join in. "Watch out young man, I'll show you how it's done," Ta would interject.

We both shared the same inherited physique. Flexing next to him showed me how I would look if I kept on my regimen. This family bonding moment usually ended as quickly as it started but not before my brother and I could break into a freestyle dance battle—Ta with house moves assisted by beat boxed audio and me with hip-hop assisted by hammer fist wall banging. Eventually, my mother realized she had something more pressing to attend to and would be the first to adjourn the session.

Amanda had time to think about my advances. She must have been thinking long about the age issue. We hadn't had a meaningful conversation in about a week and a half. I figured we would talk soon or I would soon forget. Either way, I kept myself busy. That following week I couldn't help but notice a distraction at school.

Janelle (Black/Teal Ken Griffey Jr.'s, her body was Craaaazy!!!) was in my homeroom class. I had her number on my petition since the previous year. I never got around to calling her, and actually, forgot her name was there. I would have definitely put her on a priority list if I had remembered. We often talked casually in our fifteen minutes of homeroom, as she did with every other boy in the class. Janelle was well developed and because of that she drew a lot of attention.

She had the body of a swimsuit model—not *Sports Illustrated* but an urban swimsuit model. Her figure reminded me of what, as a young man, I would want in my future. I'd seen women in their 30's that couldn't hold a candle to Janelle in that department.

Unfortunately for her, this gift came with a curse. Because of her well-developed proportions (height, lips, deceivingly experienced smile, perky breasts with stimulated nipples, flat stomach, invisible waist, and an ass that could make sitting on concrete comfortable) most guys would approach her for all the wrong reasons—just to fuck! I mean, that's the same reason I went for her number, before I realized this mannequin had feelings. It didn't hurt that she was fly in general, coordinated from head to toe in her daily wardrobe. Not Macy's fly, but Bloomys, Barneys, Jeffreys fly. Based on her accessories I wanted to assume she wore matching sets. My imagination said aqua with purple polka dots.

Knowing what bait the *catch* likes would make it easier for a gift-giving wolf (might I add? belongs to a different pack from myself). She could have been anything in life. Maybe a NASA engineer, specializing in statistic calibration diagnostics but those damn wolves didn't give her a chance to explore that side of her genius. They made her fully aware of her prized processions. Because of this constant reminder, she valued her assets for their advantage. Unfortunately, inner beauty wasn't highlighted. If the fruit looked ripe to the eye it was going to be picked. If the calf looked well fed, the chopping block prepared for veal. Guys can be relentless. I approached Janelle as a vegan, not interested in her tenderloins. No need to be predictable. Most guys my age were indirectly obvious about their intentions, never changing the angle.

Hey fellas!!! You ever thought about saying something like this? "How is your day going?" Catch her off guard, because she'd never expect that you'd be more interested in the trials of her day over your own courting attempts. "Who me?" "Yeah you. And not your school day, I'm referring to your free thoughts." Janelle looked interested in the seldom request to reflect on her day.

Distracted minds never thought of things so simple. This provided a non-judgmental open forum. Her answer couldn't be wrong. It wasn't required to be right, only a reflection of her feelings in regards to her day. She told me how she felt and I really wished I could have paid attention but that fitted white button-up had even the homeroom teacher distracted. Hey! If Mr. Cowinns snuck on-the-low professional peeks, I didn't feel too bad. "One more time please. I kind of got side tracked by a ummm late homework assignment I just remembered."

She had to know the effects of a woman's choice in button-up shirts. One button unbuttoned says: "I'm stuffy. My neck needs to breathe. I'm still serious, look at me that way." Two buttons undone says: "I really don't need to look this professional. I want you to take me seriously but don't let the set up fool you." Three buttons undone said: "I could've worn an entirely different shirt but this one allows me to taper my seduction if need be. And yes, I need you to take me seriously but I don't mind if you get sidetracked by my breasts, I mean my style." Like I said before, Janelle was fashionable, so half of our conversation was lost in her *style*.

With my hook loosely caught in her gills, I decided not to reel her in—not yet. I wanted to let that one incubate. Besides, my hook wasn't the only lure there. I recognized some *worms* (guys), *Valentine's cards* (super lames) and *Cashier's checks* (Tricks) but Tug-of-War was never a big game for me as a kid. I did run the risk of losing my catch all together but if I did, screw it. The ocean was vast and what species only has one specimen?

After school, I walked Janelle to her train station. It was the same way as my usual route. My alpha-numeric pager could be felt vibrating through my jacket pocket when I gave her my parting hug. "I think that's you," she said. "Oh, for a second there I thought I was making your heart skip," I responded back. We both laughed. "Thanks for walking me to my train. I'll see you tomorrow," Janelle said as she descended the subway stairs. I took one more professional peek thinking to myself, "Hot Damn!"

I retrieved my pager, looked at the number, and saw that it was Amanda. Though it didn't catch me off guard, it was the last thing on my mind. I was right, aside from her daily activities; she did take time to think about my advances. I called her back from the nearest pay phone.

Amanda: "Hello."
Me: "Peace!"
Amanda: "Who begins a phone conversation like that?"
Me: "You never heard someone say 'Peace' before?"
Amanda: "Oh! I thought you said 'speak'."
Me: "Nah, but that's not a bad idea. I might have to start answering like that. What's good though? How have you been? SPEAK!"
Amanda: "Are you ready for me?"
Me: "When?"
Amanda: "Now!"

Me: "Umm Sure! I'm already half way home. I'll drop off my books and then head your way."

I walked home thinking that Amanda had finally come around. As far as I was concerned she had been sort of written off. It felt like forever since our last discussion. My reaction was different now, something was unfamiliar. In my head, the whole ordeal was somewhat theatrical (almost like a monologue).

House lights dim. Blacked out stage. A spotlight slowly illuminates, while I make my way to center marker.

Yeah, we ran a few practice plays but nothing outside the scrimmage. I threw a few Hail Mary's at the end but was almost certain there wasn't a receiver that far out. I never showed or expressed any doubt in my conviction. The certainty of my words was the certainty of that future memory. Possibility was replaced with probability. If turned into When. When turned into Now. My pager hummed.

Now that I think about it, I was caught off guard. I just met my opposition. Fierce in the ring, I remained poised, delivering crushing blow after crushing blow (charm and wit). Undaunted by her form; the banner of impregnability, I kept on. It was resilient barbarism, maniacal elegance, I was a sophisticated mercenary. No, I did not stay to see my victim fall. When I walk away from explosions, I don't turn around to see the fire—It's cooler that way. I wasn't certain she was a victim, wasn't certain of her collapse.

I did what I do best and put the thoughts out there. I retired to my quarters, but not in my attempts. It wasn't until now, until that phone call, did I receive the message from the judges, applauding my performance, noting my valor and congratulating me on my success. "You might not have witnessed it for yourself, but you did win. Come collect your just due."

At this point, my "Patience" and "Conviction" had their first falling out and had temporarily parted ways. It is with solace, love, and great admiration that my Patience cannot accept this award without Conviction by his side. That was the first time in my life that I didn't step up to the plate when it was my turn at bat. A story never told.

I never went to Amanda's place that day. I never spoke to her again. I had all the intentions of going but when I arrived home I lost my motivation. Did my nerves get the better of me? Was I unsure of the outcome that I so boastfully predicted? The problem here was far greater than not seeing her. This event hindered my ability to reason my fought for actions. Was I pursuing just for pursuing sake?

Perplexed by Conviction's decision, I was left with the motive of causality when the effects are exactly what I want but my reaction is not. Threatened by a psychological diamond that has revealed another facet not positioned in the light. Examining myself; a spectrum of brilliance magnified, revealing inclusions. If I were to rewind the process: Now came from when, when came from if. If "F" (flawless) had a speck. It has now become internally flawed. (When gem terminologies enter your subconscious.) In simple terms, I chickened out and wasn't sure why.

Fade to black.

Chapter 6

The sun is always bright, especially above the clouds. It's a constant you can count on. If it were possible for the sun not to be bright, it wouldn't be the sun anymore. It would be an imposter. Anything other than you is not yourself; it is a glitch in reality. In a physical change, the properties remain the same. Easy deductive reasoning will reveal a cookie crumb trail to its genesis. Most people are who they have always been. Others might have taken longer to become themselves. In a chemical change the properties evolve, but they are not cultured. They do not acclimate themselves to their generation, nor to the heritage of their lineage.

When a linear odyssey embarks on a chemical folk, those in motion become different travelers. Rip a piece of paper in half and notice two pieces of paper. Burn a plastic cup and notice something not quite like plastic. Its form can no longer toast to your homage. Some people don't change for the better. They just change. Maturity can be subjective. My mind wanders whenever I'm on a plane. It must be that bright sunlight.

Sunday, February 8th—American Airlines seat 26 row C—a window seat with extended leg room by request. The complimentary gray headphones were irritating my ears. And why does the treble have to be so high? Where's a Bose headset when you need one? Leg room is ok, but what about side room, Jesus! Who designed this thing? The La-Z-Boys are probably in first class. Deep breaths; relax, relate, release. Sometimes you can wake up on the wrong side of the airplane chair. I glanced over a *Source* magazine that I had started reading earlier. After that, my curiosity left me analyzing some of my fellow passengers.

Hmmm, he should have known that stew chicken was a bad idea, even if we did just leave the West Indies. Caribbean cuisine taste so much different once airplane microwaved. He squirmed in his seat like a toddler with a tummy ache. I was glad I wasn't near the bathroom because when that volcano erupts the villagers won't know what hit them. His wife sat beside him, calm and reserved. They both looked to be in their late 40's. Facial wrinkles displayed time's half court pressure. There were no birds on board but crow's feet were visible.

The constant battle for armrest control and the slight bickering before reconciliation suggested the acceptance of their relationship. She was wearing a peach velour tracksuit and matching New Balance 996's. He had on knee faded dad jeans and a frayed maroon polo shirt, topped off with a paisley fedora and open toe sandals. I'm not one to call the cops but I wouldn't mind the fashion police giving out some citations on this one.

I went back to my window where I tested my creativity. I closed my eyes, centered my thoughts and then cleared them from the vestibule of my mind. I opened my eyes and upon the first cloud sighted, I would dissect its form and pair it with the recollection of something tangible, something believable. Maybe a face, a tool, an action, a script in a dialog of moving parts. A revolution admiring one notion, a full moon on a visible night and the varied impressions from a thousand onlookers. This is how it feels to be light-headed. My opulent imagination left me with many known forms from that single cloud. At that point, thoughts became weightless.

You know you see things differently when you see things differently every time you look. I understood my reasoning. I saw the structure in confusion and tried to organize what seemed like the confused part. Some people call it eccentric. Those clouds had a chaotic order. Condensed mist sometimes reminds me of a joke. A pilot walks in an airport bar and says, "Let me get a Life Raft on the rocks." The bartender looks up and says, "Funny, I never heard of that drink, what's in it?" The pilot says, "Four parts vodka, one part tequila, a splash cranberry, lemon zest, bitters and me and my next flight crew if you serve it to me neat." This is what sunlight can do to you. Half of me still admired a puff of air.

Being reminded of my eye's sweet tooth, my attention passed over that fedora; pass his aisle to the other row. I was trying to get her attention. There was always a new her. I nonchalantly leaned forward as if I was reaching to tie my Trinomics. I could smell the coconut oil in hair from my seat. Her Billie Holiday-esque gardenia was turned in the other direction. Two more attempts for her attention and I was done. Either that, or I would look like the guy who couldn't tie his own shoes.

She didn't see me at first. I had to take a break anyway, looking in her direction forced me to look at this guy again and he must've forgotten how to use a napkin. I wanted to slap him with some handy-wipes. The side of his face was making me queasy. The corner of his mouth looked like he was bobbing for apples in a tub full of gravy. "Hey, you kinda have something on your cheek." "Oh, ah, um, thanks kid," he politely responded. Distracted by his voice, she noticed me. She was aware of my presence or at least the fixation with my lo-top Pumas that I kept reaching for. I smiled and then mimed to her with my hands to write her number down. She shook her head, no. I mimed a shocked look. I then mimed a single tear that had fallen from my face onto my lap. Disheartened by my tear I looked to her, crushed and saddened.

She smiled back while reaching into the pocket of the seat in front of her. The one containing the evacuation manual and "The don't panic when it's time to panic" procedures. She took out a magazine and tore out a page. She began to write and when done, neatly folded that paper. She passed the note across the aisle to the Peach and asked her to pass it to me. The Peach handed it to the hat. "I remember when I was your age. I see things haven't changed," he reminiscently said as he handed me the note. "Is that how you met your wife, through note exchanges?" I thought I'll ask. "Not at all kid," he leaned in closer making our conversation more personal.

"My frat brothers and I came down here for carnival about fifteen years back. We had a blast—played mas and everything. We even arrived early enough to catch the Pan finals. The Mrs. loves her some steel pan. Best time of my life. We had so much fun, that in the process, I managed to knock her up. Luckily for me, it was love at first sight. We mesh well. She comes from good stock. Her family lives back in the states. We even studied under the same major. I decided to make an honest woman out of her. She was about to have my child. Don't get it twisted son, I am happily married but my risky story is rare. A few of my old fraternity brothers weren't so fortunate. They can't stand their wives." He controls his chuckles, then laughs out loud, "Make sure you use that glove, kiddo." I laughed too, thinking to myself, who says glove anymore?

"What are you talking about? What glove?" his wife interjected. "Oh, nothing Cherry Blossom, just telling the boy he can't go outfield without a glove. You know, baseball talk." She nods to him like 'yeah, ok'. Turning back to me, he winked. I winked back. That dude was pretty cool, but I still didn't want to be anywhere near that restroom when his bubble guts erupts.

I took the note and put it in my pocket. I returned to staring aimlessly out my window. I stayed in character for about five seconds before I turned back towards her. "I'm just playing," I said silently. I knew she was watching, waiting for me to read it. I took the note back out of my pocket, unfolded it and read:

You are pretty funny. Were you miming? I can't give you my number for two reasons. 1. I'm kind of seeing someone at the moment and 2. You could be a stalker. But I'll take yours if you like. My name is Theresa.

With enough space for my response, I began writing. I finished my thought and folded the paper into smaller halves then previously given. "Pardon me Mr." "Call me Keith," he says. "Can you pass this note back to Princess Jasmine over there?" "Sure! No problem, kiddo."

The note went to the Peach and back to the princess. Her Indian bloodline was strikingly apparent. Ginger and red oak coalesced and created her complexion. Her turquoise teardrop earrings and silk floral scarf displayed an elegant fashion (White and Rainbow 95 Airmax). I couldn't really make out her figure from her seated position but from the stomach up she was carefully wrapped eye candy. I watched her face as she opened my note:

ETERNAL BAKR

To Princess Jasmine a.k.a. Ms. Holiday, Nice! I think it's wonderful that you found someone special, I am happy for you but I really wasn't looking for a relationship or to disrupt yours after the first glance. I strongly believe that we come into each other's lives for a reason and I wanted your number to find out if that reason was to my benefit or yours (smiley face). As far as stalkers go, take a quick look at me.

(She turns toward me. I, then, pose in the expression of my favorite Malcolm X portrait, pondering with a closed hand on my face and pointer finger reaching for the temple. She smiled and returned to her read).

If that doesn't convince you, then I don't know what other mime to show you. But in all seriousness, I couldn't be a stalker. I hate fan clubs, unless it's my own. Tell you what, we should exchange numbers. But, I won't call you until you call me...and call me...and call me...so much that the operator just connects you straight to me as soon as you pick up the phone;) That way everything will be on your terms.

P.s. If we keep passing notes, I'm gonna have to pay this couple a postal charge for carrying my letters.

"Ladies and gentlemen we will be landing shortly. A flight attendant will be passing by with a receptacle for any trash that needs to be disposed of. Everyone please return to your seats, fasten your seat belts, return your trays and chairs to their upright position. The current temperature in New York City is 47 degrees Fahrenheit. The captain and crew would like to thank you for flying American Airlines and we hope that you will choose us again for your future travel needs."

Walking through the airport corridor I told my brother about the stew chicken, the glove, and Princess Jasmine. "Jasmine works better with curry you know?" he clowned. He was seated further up front with one of my other brothers, my mother, and two of my sisters. I could have changed my seat to sit with the family but that would have meant me giving up my window. My first trip to visit my grandmother in the Caribbean left me stuck in the aisle. Getting my elbow bumped by every bathroom goer didn't need to be repeated.

During the taxi ride home, we all shared tropical stories. My mother had her rum and coke narrative, my sisters had their virgin daiquiri tales, me and my next brother up had our soda pop adventures and my oldest brother on the trip had his *Shandy* sagas. He also had a sequel, "King Ding-a-ling and the Crusade of the Smut Puppets," but that's a different memoir.

Our first and only legit family vacation proved to be very memorable for everyone. Is it me or do vacations always become better right before you have to leave? The after-hype of the experience hadn't begun to die down yet. We all had stories of new friends, secluded hangouts and adventures. Mine wouldn't be forgotten quickly. I brought my mountain bike along for the trip. As soon as we touched dirt, I assembled it, eager to explore the landscape. I rode off into the sunset and quickly learned that steep cliffs, hill sides, speeding trucks, narrow two-way streets, opposite side of the street traffic and a small aluminum frame would either boost my confidence or kill me.

To this day I never told my mother how close I came to being pulled into the vortex of a speeding vehicle or going over cliff side. At the time, I didn't want to worry her, but knowing my mother, she would have said, "Just be careful" or "You know your limits better than I do." Besides the interest in girls, that kind of stuff is what young boys do and my mother was a passive endorser of young men taking part in manly activities. She was hip.

Thirty-five minutes of vacay highlights and we were back home. The airport was now a part of a montage of memories. My mother walked in the house first and told us to retrieve the bags and tip the cabbie. My brother told her he'd take care of it. "Don't drive down dark alleys, sir." We all enjoyed that one. With a new tan, one of my Hawaiian shirts and a beaded necklace that I picked up from a roadside local, I was ready for my favorite pastime. Girls!

I made a few calls.

Me: "Hey girl, I'm back in town."
Mali: "Who? Who is this?"
Me: "You would think when a girl gets swept off her feet, she would remember it for a lifetime."
Mali: "No really, who is this?"
Me: "No really, you would really think when a girl gets swept off her feet she would remember that dashing gentleman who was able to put a rose in his mouth without being pricked by the thorn."
Mali: "Now I definitely don't know who this is."

Me: "Jesus, it's me dammit! Ok. I'll help. You were out about two weeks ago. You were watching a school football game. Periwinkle and fuchsia pink Diadoras and a matching Benetton jacket, if memory serves me correctly. Looking fly like you probably always do. I imagine every jerk with moving lips was trying to run game, telling you how pretty you are and how they like your hair, and those jeans look nice on you and my name is blah, blah, blah, bubble gum, bubble yum. Then out of nowhere, the ref blew the whistle, the game stopped, the cheerleaders sprang into action and I emerged out of the melee, tapped you on the back and said..."

Mali: "Oh! Of course. You said, 'Act like you know me because my boy set me up on a blind date and I just saw her. Hell to the no.' You know I had to tell my girlfriend about that. How did that situation turn out for you anyway?"

Me: "What do you mean? After I left you, I dipped. As far as I was concerned, you were the most important part of the game. After I saw you I couldn't imagine there being a better highlight."

Mali: "You're funny. I see your one of those guys. "

Me: "Are you that quick to judge?"

Mali: "No! But I ain't new to this and you look the part, attractive, well dressed, aware of your appearance, very personable, fast talker, and..."

Me: "Hold up counselor. I talk fast because I think fast. My mother had all of my siblings and I attached to *Hooked on Phonics*. You know, child development!"

Mali: "Ok, that semi-explains the fast talking but you know what I mean..."

Me: "Yeah, I know what you mean. You should give me a chance to clear my name. Let me paint you a picture. You're a little girl, very little. Your mother has been giving you precious jewels all your life. Let's call those jewels, money. Every week you put that money in your memory bank. Let's call that memory bank, the piggy bank. Weeks turn into months, months turn into years and you have learned to appreciate your mother's heirlooms. You deposit them faithfully. They are cherished in your piggy bank. One sunny Saturday afternoon your mother and you walk through the park. The air is cool. Frisbee is now a winter sport. Two and a half feet of freshly fallen snow cushions the sole of young daring acrobats.

ETERNAL BAKR

Little grown Mali is wearing that red crochet hat with the attached cat ears. You love that red hat. While in the park, your mother asked you, 'Would you like some hot chocolate sweetie - with extra whip cream, maybe a piece of warm banana bread too? I know it's your favorite.' You happily agree.

On y'alls way to Ms. Cozy's Bakery, you and your mother are approached by a man. He is bundled up tightly, wearing a black jacket, black gloves, black skully and a black ski mask. This man is firm in his request. He wants what y'all have. All you wanted was banana bread. You guys never made it to Ms. Cozy's that afternoon. Your mother was robbed and along with her pocketbook your piggy bank went too!"

Mali: "Wowww, that's quite an imagination you have there!!!"
Me: "Not done yet. Years go by and young Mali has bloomed into a sought-after perennial. Her girlfriends are all graduating high school this particular year and wanted to do something as a collective before their future at different colleges. They decide to take a trip to Aspen. Eager to hit the slopes, your girls want to start off light, but this isn't your first trip to Colorado and the bunnies won't do. While most of your friends take the novice route, young Mali has decided to venture into the advanced section. Snug in her Bogner, eyes in her Oakleys and fastened tightly in her Salomons, she is ready to kick off. But wait, at the top of the hill she is momentarily paralyzed. Her poles drop down to the freshly fallen. Her guard goes up. Young Mali sees ME on the slopes wearing a black jacket, black gloves, black skully and black ski mask. Traumatic events of the past rush in as she remembers the discomfort, the safety that was once stolen from her, along with that piggy bank. All those weeks, all those years, all those deposits, way too many to count. She thinks to herself, 'Could this be happening all over again?' No, I am not that same guy. I like to match and I just came here to ski."

Mali: (silence)

Me: "You still with me?"
Mali: "You are over the top. Wow!!! You are either going to be really good at something good or really good at something bad. I hope you choose the good path. I understand your point but I am not here for your practice."
Me: "Ha! Nah, you're definitely not practice material. Someone like you gets framed and placed on your own shelf."
Mali: "Yeah, my own shelf. But there's probably a library in the next room. I might have some space to frame you though!"
Me: "Whoa! Now who's the collector? Side note, where did your name come from? Region?"
Mali: "Well, my father is an anthropologist and my mother is an electrophysiologist."
Me: "Afros and Electric slide what?"
Mali: "Silly! Anyway, both their jobs had them pinned down in labs and libraries so much so, that whenever they had vacation time they would do a lot traveling abroad. Before I came in the picture, my parents visited Port-au-Prince in Haiti, Osaka Japan, Moscow, Cali—not the west side but the city in Columbia, Tibet, Paris, Taipei, Kuala Lumpur, New Delhi, Cairo, Casablanca, Johannesburg and few other places but Timbuktu was their absolute favorite. It was also their last stop before coming back stateside. And guess where Timbuktu is? Mali! It's actually my middle name."

That was the typical nature of our conversations. They were fun, fresh, yet revealing. Along with my usual agenda and team roster, Mali was ascending the ranks quickly.

Unbeknownst to her, she was making me question the relevance of some of my other team players. Do I really need a half back if my running back is so dominant? Is a point guard necessary if my shooting guard could run the floor? Relationships have their beauty, so does the single life. The constant in each is the void that the other leaves behind. She was sharp. I wasn't new to sharp, but this was different. She was equipped to handle my sport—insightful enough to see me coming and strong enough to hold her ground. This was genuine. Like a good defense attorney, she made me spend time when establishing my position. She was an aggressor in her own right.

Car collections are a little less meaningful when you fancy your daily driver (the options are less appealing when you have a favorite). Sooner or later you stop paying the Esurance (attention). You might let a friend take a joy ride (have a chance because you appreciate the value and understand the term *sharing is caring* is truly underrated). You might end up relinquishing the title to a collector who has been waiting for the chance to upgrade (you realize your treasure could be their shrine as they wait for your break up or involvement). "That's ok pal, no exchange necessary. You don't have anything I want. It's yours. Take it. Hopefully, if and after you grow out of it, you'll pass it along to the next (relationships). My maturity scares me. The maturity of her discernment excites me.

Mali: "I thought about inviting you over to meet my parents, but I don't know if I'm ready for that yet."
Me: "Why would I want to meet your parents? They perform magic tricks?"
Mali: "No, they don't perform magic tricks, but I know you wanna meet my parents. And the mere fact that I even brought this up says I like you a little more than I did yesterday."

Me: "I already knew you liked me more yesterday when you accepted my chewed gum. I bet you're still wondering how it still had flavor? If a family meeting is the sign of acceptance and you really want to show me how much you care, take me to the gravesite of your great grandparents." (She laughs)
Mali: "And wouldn't you like that. That won't work though. They were cremated but maybe if we get a Ouija Board, you can ask for their approval."

She definitely had some slick comebacks. Our convos went everywhere; from history to science, religion, pop culture and sometimes just sexual innuendos (Hey, I was still a teenager.) It all flowed. I never once had to lie to her. And she never once asked me any questions that would warrant one. Our untitled titles had no jurisdiction over such questions. She was personable over the phone and distractingly striking in person, beautiful without reservation.

Being with Mali reminded me of how it all began. My strategy had evolved since my first crush. All those encounters showed me how to sharpen my claws. I struck when the iron was hot and even struck when it wasn't just for the reactions. From confident to cognizant. More often than not, people do what's natural. Before Mali, things were naturally easy. I'm not saying that I met my equal, however, a compliment accentuates the whole.

With little effort I sparred, but you have to incorporate a different level of skill when your sparring partner has some training. I couldn't just run *any* fast talk with her. And, if I did, I would have to make sure it was packed with substance and findings just in case she questioned my sources. She helped me evolve and become more competent in my interactions with women of her caliber.

For half a second I felt remorse for the girls I'd dealt with prior. I almost regretted using them for what seemed like practice. But that's what cats like me did until we were comfortable, until we were bored or distracted by a new string. Sympathy was not a learned virtue. A young man with a cold heart was not necessarily considered a bad thing in my era. It was respected and secretly admired. Just think, the other side to that persona was being a sucker for love, and who knowingly wants the blind spot that tags along with that? And for the other half of that second, I didn't feel any remorse for the informed. Knowing what I was capable of, most girls I dealt with still entertained my advances.

Cold didn't mean cold-hearted exactly—it was synonymous with strength. Some guys just projected it wrong. It is possible to isolate that side of your personality so that you don't come off as a dick—if, you know your audience. And if you know your audience, you know what they came for. Those seeds were planted for cultivation, no need to manipulate the earth when you can grow from it.

Again, my values had evolved, but no regrets can be given to the past. The foundation was set, exposing the inner workings of the game and all its mindfuckery. Learned behavior will favor those who learn it first. In hindsight, I don't think I was necessarily faster than any of my peers, I just feel I had a head start in the courting process. Which stems from exposure and all those early male influences.

To be worldly, you should want to explore, but explore with an open mind because one transaction is not enough prep for the market. No one testimony can entirely ascribe life's essence. Knowing what you don't like, helps you define what do like. As egocentric as it may sound, options for a person with particular taste is based on need not greed. If you will allow me to submerge in thought for a second, the chrysalis of collection is filtration. I won't downplay how enjoyable the amassment part is but what you extract in the end should trump it all. (Ha! you just said trumpet without a music reference.)

The world is vast and our understanding will ferment with time. Every encounter has become a stepping stone responsible for my height. From that apex, I over-stood that everyone's allure is based on viewer discretion. Her eyes will set on something. So, if not me or you, she has to like somebody. Like begets the possibility of hope. Hope, the source of perseverance. And perseverance; dedicated to the idea, the possibility of what we like, becoming what we have. Projection manifested.

They say a woman can tell the second she meets you whether or not she fancies the idea of intimacy. I challenge those women to figure out, in that same second, if her counterpart genuinely feels the same way. Not just the intimacy part but the meaningful stuff. If answered early and correctly, we just cut out half the fluff (games) in dating. I knew most didn't know at first, so guys like me, liked to navigate the gray area. One man's fog is another man's atmosphere. Not that visibility was obstructed in this pairing, I knew Mali would fall for me. Knowing what she brought to the table, I fell with her. It's either we like what we have or have what we like.

We remember this memoir mirrored in the reflection of my first love and the figurative speed dating rounds I had to endure to find her. I'll be with you again swinging in the hammock of our bloom. Maybe....I can only hope. I have to like somebody. And when I find you—when I find you on the best day of the week, during the best weather of the day, right in front of my face. Before we lose ourselves, leaning against a wall with no barriers. Before we fall in and out of something we could have walked through. Before our favorites become customs and customs perquisites.

ETERNAL BAKR

Before I remember that you like little random stories before bedtime and your hair stroked like a spoiled feline. Before you remember how I like my stories told like theatrical stage plays or how I like to stare into your eyes when we dine, looking to translate your feelings through the softness of your expression, before you burn my food, before I'm late to our engagement. Before we grow old together.... tell me.... what is....

Me: "…your first name?"
Mali: "Samyra."

Chapter 7

    I assumed I should easily overpower her. After all, we were play wrestling. I found myself using real tactics to get her into submission moves. Not sure if I was embarrassed by my lack of superiority or impressed by the presence of hers. She swung for my face. "Oh no honey!" This was about to get dangerous. I ducked in stunning fashion and struck twice to let her know that her reaction needed to be more proactive—one tap to her abs, one tap to her shoulder. "Samyra!" (Sah-my-rah) I love saying her name.

    "Don't start nothing you can't finish," I pleaded, at the same time antagonizing her with spirit fingers. She used to be a cheerleading captain (go figure). Unhappy with my taunts, she rushed in. I accepted the tackle. Her skin feels like time's first step. The back of her shirt ruffles free from her pants exposing the angel wing tattoo on the small of her back.

    "Wanna see me make an angel fly?" "What?" she replied. I then smacked her ass with enough force to make it sting. She immediately jumps free from my grasp. "It almost flew. Let me try again." She is not happy with my style of play. I am bitten. "You bitch!" I mean it in a good way. I knew she wouldn't let that smack slide but I was caught in a vulnerable state, dazed and confused by those hips—straight from the luau, Samyra's complexion was like Kahlua. Her skin: like spring's first petal. I see she doesn't mind playing rough. I toss aside what's left of my mangled shirt. "Someone here is sure to bruise babe, and I don't think it's going to be me. I like you better in long sleeve shirts anyway, gives me something to think about."

    She wasn't amused. She planned her next offense by going back to the tackle. We grapple standing. She pinches my lower back. "Ah, ah, ahhh! Sorry honey, no fat there and my muscles have stretched the skin. That's not effective." "I wonder how your muscles deal with this," she says while pinching that same area with the tips of her fingernails. "Ohh, that's cheating. Ok, that's how you want it?" I placed one foot behind her and pushed. She would have fallen on her own but she grabbed my belt buckle with one hand and never let go of my ribbed tank top with the other.

    Say goodbye to vertical as we land on the couch. Spring coils help the trampoline. The back of her head making friends with the armrest, she yells "Oww!!" The play stops. I felt the impact of her trauma. The reverberation went through the cushion to the wood skeleton of the sofa. "Are you ok? You know I didn't do that on purpose. Let me see. I'll kiss it for you." "Don't touch me," she says as she curls in isolation. "You see, that's why I don't like playing like this. I knew your dainty ass was going to get hurt. Let me see! Make sure it's not bad." I took a knee by the side of the couch to get a closer look. "Move! I got this." I try to free her hands from covering her face but she's set in her decision.

    I came in closer to review the point of impact. My hands moved ever so lightly as they scanned her crown. I suddenly learned why her hands concealed her expression. She didn't have a poker face in her arsenal. Just when I was close enough to strike, she took advantage of my sympathy. Smiling from the success of her deception, she jumped on top of me. "Gotcha!" She celebrates by biting my lip. I need my bottom lip. I'm waiting for its release so I can return the favor. Say goodbye couch, as we tumble to the floor. One by one, each petty bite turns into petty kisses in the discourse. "Let me kiss where it hurts." "It hurts all over," she whispered.

The fine line between aggression and passion are smeared. We are clearly headed to the other side of the grill, the side under the steel, closer to the flame. We never stopped kissing. Like soft pillows, that refuse to stack properly, forcing cohesion, the kisses continued. Searching for that special spot, I was so comfortable, only to remember that life would be better if I could get to that condom, which was tucked away in the fifth pocket of my blue jeans.

I always wondered what was the purpose of the fifth pocket? The carriage for my Trojan horse must have been created for another purpose because when the first pair of Lees came out, most of society rode bareback. I'm going for it. The tailor in me wants to sew something together but it has to be seamless. Reaching for a condom to put in a better position for later has to flow effortlessly.

Our lips are in dialog with a tongue interpreter, objecting violently, distracting attention from my two-finger execution. Her bra cascades down the wall. I tossed it there, condemned for lunacy, for concealing the bosom of her sexuality. Her breasts could feed a nation but I'm the only one present. We are free, floating in the absence of presence, timeless in our motion. Every second counts, every heartbeat sets the cadence. A glimpse, a glance to glare—blinded by anticipation. Everything done with our eyes closed and still clothed. We enact our desires like rehearsing a screenplay.

The perfect kiss: moist and smooth. We go in on an angle. The blood rushes to the surface of her lips in search of a better seat in the house, front row to a magic show, making her red lipstick obsolete. Timed and soft, our tongues sweep the bottom half of the pair making this the most gratifying collision ever recorded. Wordless speech, a collage of thoughts easily understood. My tongue, still mine, ready for its introduction, slowly glides from backstage, past the props, and gently opens the curtains. Facing her theater, she does the same. We acquaint ourselves, matter over mind, and then mind returns altered as I realize her mouth tastes like the syrup of mangos.

The perfect touch: gentle pressure and misdirection of my intentions, moments of what could be, must first be identified. Security clearance, a must, as my hands welcomingly probe her body. Always sure to spend more time in her vaginal region because my sensors detect elevated temperature there. We are pulled in, magnetized by each other's heat. Her skin is now her best friend, sure to run back and report to her everything felt. Feels like strobe lights because at this current, electricity is erratic. She's surprised by what she sees when touch replaces her vision. Let's make the movie better. I feel like I'm seven years old. She looks like a playground; my playground. Kids love sprinklers. She smells like home and I'm drawn to baked secrets on her window sill. The aroma invites me.

She grabs my pants, unhappy with their construction. "You never hated buttons before." Disgruntled with security of zippers. Finally off, they are now intimate with her bra. Thrown on top, those pants still seem to have the upper hand. One by one, we continue to disrobe—rhythms induced. Every article unbuttoned, unzipped, unraveled, un-tied, unlaced and undone. Samyra removes the bobby pins from her bun. The volume of her hair dances on her shoulders eager to go with the flow.

The floor is covered with our belongings: blue jeans, white top, pink blouse, gray pants, white socks, white gold wrist watch, yellow gold bangles, her name plate necklace, amethyst studs and crimson red boxers. I let her keep her green thong on, for now. Two seconds away from my birthday wish to be in our birthday suits. We take one of those seconds to pause, possessed by the spirit of awareness.

"If I never make love again, I want this to be the blueprint." Let them mummify our act, to be unearthed a thousand years later, just to see that no fossilized carbon copy can remake what's made. We are about to make history. Let our entry fulfill the past with wonderment. I swear things will never be the same. Samyra's eyes are misty. I share her sentiments. I could hear them now "The mold was broken. The factory shut down. The designer, architect and engineer have vanished." Schematics on papyrus. Please don't touch—your fingerprints might smudge perfection.

I lay on top. She remained in a welcoming position. Her dark brown hair tangled by the floors friction, shoulders pinned loosely. The sigmoid shape of her spine elevates her lower back just high enough for me to remember why we're different. My arms straight, bracing the weight of my desires. My neck, my chest, deep breaths hollowed by the grunt of my bravado. My elbows ease. I take her hand with mine and pull it behind her head with our fingers interlocked. I'm closer. Her lips puckered. Her eyes fixate to mine. Her mouth is open.

The warm air of her breath sends cool chills throughout my body. I hope I'm doing the same. Closer, closer, closer to her ear, I whisper nothing. I whisper nothings. I speak to her lobe, "Everything tastes like honey." My body rises from the height of her goose bumps all while gyrating the footnotes to the coming attraction. Energy changes form. I want to flood her thoughts in hopes that the transference will saturate her immortal portal. It's working. If I don't rescue her seafoam green panties now, they are sure to be submerged.

Awakened by tension, we open our eyes and relax to the sight of beauty. Our body heat could turn liquid into vapor. I stand up, and then I stand her up and carry her to the bedroom. Only a trench coat could hide my excitement and even then, the crowd would still think this guy was packing. Picking her up by cupping her ass, her legs wrap and lock around my waist like I possess the last parachute. We're in this together. She wants to fall with me. We head to the master bedroom. The bed has a canopy and this picture deserves a frame.

 Still securely fastened to the trunk of my body, we stop before the canopy's nylon screen entrance. I tell her, "Look at me. Remember my eyes. Remember this place. This place is you. You are where I go to between my thoughts. On days when my body is too weary to move, I will escape my encapsulated host and venture alone, just to visit the idea of you." The bedroom has no walls. Well, it might but I don't wish them there. The nylon is brushed aside as we descend on the pillow top mattress. Our auras replace the glow of the candles; the candles melt before being lit. The canopy twirls like a carousel. The pillows are pushed aside for this royal procession.

 Noble, yet possessive in my manner, I clench the back of her hair and pull down until her neck is exposed. I take a full second to visually admire before my sense of touch exudes jealousy. Soft feather kisses, light toffee touches, my hands explore her body like new terrain to a journeyman.

 A single trail blazed from toe to summit. I kiss one half and bite the other. I stop at her stomach. This is where I set up camp. I acquaint myself with her naval base. I place my face on her stomach, touching my cheek to her skin before my lips follow suit. Making my way down the hallway of her thigh I am reminded of her angel wings. "Hey babe, you wanna know what an angel feels like?" Intrigued by my next action, her eyes roll from left to right as she nods in favor.

 Samyra's seafoam is more like hunter green as I remove her wet panties. Her legs spread open reserving space for my solo performance. My biceps, locking her into position as my hands surface around her thighs, pressing hard enough on her soft flesh to leave indentations. Engulfed with the scent of that honey and mango syrup, the perfect kiss is center stage again. Past the props and theatrical lighting, the curtain opens. Soft pink and glistening with sensitivity, my lips, freshly licked, open hers and my tongue glides past her labia in an effort to elate her clitoris, lustful in my monologue. Samyra, looking for something to hold on to, reaches for the headboard. She braces for control with a vice-like clutch, clenched so hard that the wood begins to splinter.

I'm not into branding but if I am going to leave a hickey anywhere it's going to be here. Her grip attempts to levy her body. My mouth disperses a smaller vessel from the ship, seeking out her spot. Soaked and wet I lay claim to a mass uncharted. Her brow crushed, cheeks pushed back and the bottom part of her forehead wrinkled. She looks like she is slowly being forced on a bed of nails while being served her favorite dessert, one spoonful at a time. She has no control here. I'm serving this dish. Her thighs are tightly bolted to my arms as I take my time exploring her new world. Lost at sea, before I re-emerge to the surface.

Samyra bites her lower lip partially revealing her pearly whites. Smiles and short breaths. Her face looks thrilled and excited. Momentary combustion at the thought of taking the heaven in her head and bringing it here to earth. I want her to feel the sweet pain of life. The gravity of her bitten lip pulls me back up, past the valley of her belly and the rounded mounds of her breast. The area of her areola, like cinnamon circles, I stop to make swirls. From there I make short candy kisses across the bridge of her neck.

I hover over her chin like air in a wind tunnel, about to pour brut in the open lip end of the funnel. Soft, pink and glistening with sensitivity, she softly kisses my head sweeping the shaft with the taste buds of her tongue. She takes her hand and gently winds this cork, twisting right up until the point of discomfort—right to the point where I want to stop her. Then quickly lets loose, and before my skin can unravel, I am swallowed whole. She is careful not to bite with the insertion. I am reaching for the same splintered grip on the head board. Deep breaths and smiles—I'm back to my wits.

My left hand firmly cuffs both of her entwined wrists. My right hand squeezes her right breast with her nipple playing peak-a-boo between my fingers. Lost in the eye of the storm, Samyra's body is about to experience the other half of the wave setting on the sun. She quivers in anticipation. I steadily lower my anchor. She takes a deep breath. At the same time, I try to fill the void in her canal with the same breath that left her lungs.

"I got you babe," her hips rotate on a different plane, the closest I'll ever get to being conjoined. Samyra, eager to compliment my setting, has changed my mental hue from a serene cream to a purple so dark that it smells like chocolate. This feels too good to be good; it has to be bad. I'm working on a picture here. Wisdom packaged in youth. I grab her knees, pushed down close to her chest like a cannonball. The legs of the bed frame are heard grinding into the wood floor, but not nearly as hard as we are grinding in the mattress—both posts looking for the groove. I'm on top, every stroke is to a different setting.

My pores open, sweat beads gradually form and run down my face just to springboard off my chin. They dive into her mouth, drip by drip. Her tongue moves like slow wiper blades over her palette. Sure to leave a lasting impression, she whispers, "I don't care where I am in life. This is yours. You can always have me. Look at me. I'm not playing, this is yours. If we ever part, find me and remind me why I said this to you. THIS IS YOURS." My ego floats away in a hot air balloon soon to be lost in the stratosphere.

No prominent pattern. No formula to what we do here. Sway...bend...dip...dive...rush...halt...slow...wind...pulsate...pulsate ...pause...dig...retreat...rush...retreat...raise...wait...wave...wait... pause...dig...dig...dig...dig...let's try a hypnotist spiral. This blueprint has extensions, erections not at their peak. My fingers turn numb. The blood retreats from this extremity and congregates to the region on the front line, engorged by the revolution. I expand, shifting the tectonic plates of her womb. She quakes. The saturated lips of center stage have taken the limelight. A moving spotlight is there to capture every nuance. "Give me a second," she says short of breath. "No, no. We'll breathe when we're done," I convince her. We are making music here; chords, flats, and sharps dance above our heads, all orchestrated by heart's chamber. Positions are thoughts and we go through them all.

I direct her to a sitting posture. We are now on the side skirt of the bed. Her firm smooth legs stretch out behind me as she straddles my saddle. Bucking violently, each wall hit, each stroke reveals a revelation, an epiphany to her sexual imagination. So swift, so changeable, Samyra displays every facial expression her muscles could muster. Her face in a blush, her hair has nowhere to go; the strands matte together. Her manicured nails dig tribal marks in my back. This is intimacy. Our bodies are pressed so firmly together that molecules suffocate. Trapped. Squeezed.

There is no place for anything else. My hands make their way under her extended legs causing their retraction. I grab the side of her back where her angel wings should have been. We stand, while in the motion, and thrust against the wall. Her eyes roll to the back of her head, unnecessary for vision. We never lose rhythm. I'm strumming every chord. Banging her back to the wall, the sound of dark notes escapes the crackling of the hollowed sheet rock. Past lust. Lust was my first crush. Paint chips color the floors…this is more, this is more like a rite of passage, an inauguration, a birth before conception. Reverb amplifies the pitch of her voice to the level of stadium speakers. The impression of the human form, we crack the surface.

She screams my name over and over, every outburst more jubilant. The wooden studs within the wall do little to support the madness of our method. We approach the bridge. We break down the beat to a single instrument, leading to that high note. The riff, the rip of the wave looking to crash—ready to extract her lungs from the cavity. I cover her mouth with my hand and tell her, "I CAN'T HEAR YOU" just so she can bite my fingers in disbelief. My tribal marks like whiskers have now stretched across my back.

The shattered spread of the wall cracks distance themselves from the epicenter of our impact. She quakes. Every sense heightened just shy of super heroism, we are beings far from human. "Samyra, I'll show you God if you open your eyes." She looks and stares at the soul of this man. I reverse polarity. "Look, a supernova in a black hole," I whisper. She watches her reflection in my iris knowing that her image can't escape. We bang the lubricated crevice, her wall. The wall is soaked in our sweat.

We fondled at the entrance, 'foreplayed' on the waiting line and became one with the steep ascent. This rollercoaster, however, doesn't have the perceived drop many are accustomed to. When we reach its highest peak, into pieces of kinetic energy. We explode, into dust. The wall collapses from our final blow, a firework of the solar system, quilted fibers weaving our matter into vapor. And what's not returned to the essence, floats like snow.

We are covered in soot and debris as our bodies were literally plastered into the wall. Forced into deep breaths and open pores, perspiration looks for the cool. We lay next to each other like two feared animals hit by tranquilizers in the height of their chase, competing for air to oxygenate the breathless. Both on our backs, I scan the room and think to myself, "Where did we just go, because I don't recognize any of this?"

That's because the living room is painted in a different shade. Covered in the remnants of war paint, I roll my head over in her direction, "You gave me everything. I gave you everything. Why are we so drained? Didn't we receive anything in the process?" "Good point," she replies. Not wanting to say too much, Samyra closes her eyes. I do the same. We both have not fully returned to our capsules.

Hours passed before any real motion was felt. Somewhere in the middle of the night we must have gotten up off the floor and returned to bed. Still covered in frosting, I held her tightly. Samyra, after waiting her turn, tried to spoon me. "Hey, I'm the guy here." "Are you hungry?" she asked. "Hell yeah!" "Would you be so kind as to get us something from the kitchen?" I thought about it. This would be the perfect way to start the morning—I'll cook us breakfast and we'll eat in bed.

Then I thought about how comfortable she appeared. I was just as comfortable. "I really don't want to get up babe. Can we odds and evens for it? Your call." She calls "Evens." "Dammit! You waited dumb long to put your finger out. That's like cheating. Let's do it over. Your call." She calls "Evens." "Dammit! I'll be right back babe. Keep my spot warm." She laughed.

I had to walk through the living room to get to the kitchen. There was a huge hole in the wall, clothes were everywhere. It looked like a house party on steroids. I located my boxers underneath the sea foam by the fireplace, two inches from the ash. How the hell did her panties get out here? To my surprise they were far from dry. I returned to the bedroom to show Samyra her wandering secrets. I found nothing but an unmade bed. She wasn't there. I knocked on the bathroom door. No answer. "It's too early for hide and seek." I went back to the living room and put on my pants, ready for another game.

I took a quick peek in the front yard. I grabbed the doorknob, turned it clockwise and pulled the door open. When attempting to run across the front yard, I fell. Now on my back thinking to myself, "What the hell? Did I slip? Did the sprinklers over water this lawn?" The strange thing was, I didn't get up immediately. Looking at the sky, I stared at the sun. The sun looks different today. It actually looks like…it looks like my ceiling light. I smiled. I never knew wet dreams were so real.

It's 1999, we're not close to floating cars yet but these new Flightposites were close enough. Only thing better than that, was the fact that I copped them in the White/Red/Black colorway. At this time, it should only be me and the St. John's College basketball team rocking them. Hahaha! It's gonna be a great day. Where's my black book? I need to live out my dreams.

-FIN-

OPEN FORUM

I thought about taking this section out, because when this memoir was written in the mid 2000s, the best place to get random thoughts were from open mic nights and poetry books. Instagram wasn't out yet. Twitter was too new and Facebook wasn't popular. Everyone was on MySpace playing their favorite music and too busy adjusting their Top 8 to impart any wisdom on their friends. But now, we are completely flooded. I'm not sure what this world has more of: quotes or assholes. (Not assholes like assholes, I mean like literal assholes, like butt holes, you get what I'm trying to say.) Even so, I decided to preserve this section with a little modification. I replaced many of my personal quotables with detailed stories. Enjoy

P.s. If a name is dropped here, it's real. P.p.s. These are already true stories but if I say "True story" during a true story that's because I need to remind you how real despite the irony or absurdity that part of the true story is.

From time to time the executives in my head conduct a roundtable meeting by the bay windows. A few wear tailored suits, the others are super casual as they divulge matters of the mind and heart. APA who? MLA what? Nothing proper, nothing politically correct. Structure-less. *Robert's Rules of Order* don't apply here. Just random memories, thoughts and observations. Take a gander. Its raw. Welcome to the *Open Forum*.

♦

Success is not getting everything you want; it's wanting everything you get.
-Unknown author (I had to add this one. Future me would appreciate it.)

◆

Ladies are Sneaker Pimps too. I met a few. Meeting a female Sneaker Pimp was like talking to another team captain. The conversation was different. They had a roster just like you.

◆

Watch out for people who laugh immediately after they talk. Not laughter after a corny joke, but laughter after any random statement. If you haven't noticed this person before, pay attention. If you're the person I'm talking about, cut it out. (A future psychoanalytical book I will never write.)

◆

Even on a crowded train, someone is sitting comfortably.

◆

Cherish your parents. Learn from them what you can while you guys still breathe the same air. Remember, respect and emulation are different. If they spent all these years on this planet and didn't gather enough stories to present you with a proper book on life, respect them. That was still time served. But if they set the example in any way, form or fashion; emulate! That's momentum for your monument.

Oh, but if they abused you and took advantage, fuck'em. Contrary to what they say, you don't have to forgive someone in order to have a clear conscience. Nice but not necessary. That's their cross to bear. Peace of mind is personal.

♦

The first time I realized age is NOT just a number. I was 7, my 16-year-old 'girlfriend', Christina, introduced me to her boyfriend.

♦

Make a difference, a positive difference, in the life of another. If not, kick rocks. Preferably with an over-supplied pair of counterfeit J's you thought were real right up until that rock you just kicked peeled back your sole.

♦

Moon Boots? C'mon ladies. Everything can't be cool.

♦

Loving you, will keep me next to you. Liking you, will let me enjoy being next to you. I'm searching for the Like of my Life.

♦

The reason some elders say "Take advantage now, life will pass you by before you know it" is because most of them don't remember getting old in the first place. Think about that for a second. Time moves slow enough where you can see it vividly but fast enough where you can forget it somewhat immediately. It is a phenomenon. Try to treat it as such. There is no rewind button. You can wish until you're blue in the face but you'll never be able turn back the hands of time. So why practice regret, you'll never get it right.

♦

Sometimes when sitting on a crowded train I have an internal debate on who I'm gonna give my comfortable seat to? Of course, my elders without hesitation. But wait, she's not old enough. Well, what about her? Who her? She needs to stand. This is probably the only exercise she is willing to do. What about him? Oh, that man, well he is a man so he has to be slightly older than old to qualify. Or he can be exempt if he shows anguish or that older man grimace face when moving.

♦

I love a beautiful clean face. I like makeup if it's simple or artistically done. I don't like makeup if it's necessary and I especially don't like it when it's on my pillows, sheets, jackets or shirts. Please ladies, acquire a product that doesn't smudge. Either that or we are going to start sharing the cleaning bill.

♦

The quickest way to e-q a sound is to lower the volume. HA! (I just gave you a life lesson. I'll send an invoice)

♦

This is copyrighted, published, digital and in print! It is over. This book was written when the stories were still fresh in my memory. Do you know how hard it was to scale down the use of the letter "I" when talking about yourself. I can tell you it wasn't easy ;). One of the things I learned though, writing gives you power. Kjnfiua woa werjn. You see! I just typed with my eyes closed and you tried to read it. When someone wants your incomplete thoughts, that's power or more correctly, that's relevance.

♦

Next time you are cold, put a scarf on.

♦

We hustled. I paid for 70% of those high school sneakers. I would've felt hella funny asking my mother for a hundred plus dollars for kicks. Her bills were real and my fashion was real superficial.

♦

I could have written this memoir while still in high school but the weather was nice.

♦

It was written shortly after college when the weather was partly sunny, partly cloudy.

◆

I once met up with a girl. Junior high school years (I.S.131, Chinatown). My boy, Freddy Cruz, was meeting up with his girl. Man, that dude was overly affectionate in public with his shorty. Hand on her ass, swapping spit every second. Like, we get it, that's all you brother. But that was my dude, my ace. That was his style. Clearly we were raised different. Anyway, back to my blind date he set me up with. She was Cool! Pretty! Good to go! And she was digging me. She probably never met a guy before with hair longer than hers. So, we hugging up on some corner in L.E.S. (Lower East Side of Manhattan). Nothing like what Freddy was doing five feet away from us. While hugging, she glanced up into my eyes. I looked back down at hers. As I admired her face, her eyes like maple, her skin tone the shade of cherry wood, lips super glossy. Her nose caught my attention. HER NOSE CAUGHT MY ATTENTION. She had a nose hair poking out of one nostril. A fucking nose hair. I thought only old people had nose hairs. This bitch is 14-years-old with an extended nose hair. What the fuck. I couldn't stop staring. How did she miss that? I know she used a mirror for all that lip gloss. Mirrors actually see for you. Damn, it was so early in our street corner date. I had to play it off for another hour. I wanted to tell them I heard my mother calling me from Brooklyn but I didn't want to leave Freddy hanging. I'll never forget that day. A MUTHAFUCKIN nose hair.

◆

For the record, adult me would never call a 14-year-old girl a bitch. 14-year-old me might, especially if she went on a date with a visible MUTHAFUCKIN nose hair.

♦

Sometimes no matter how sunny it is outside; everything feels dreary and gloomy.
Nothing seems to work in my favor. Sometimes I want to change my own skin, cut off all my hair and disappear. And then I do my laundry and everything feels better.

♦

You know you're shopping in an expensive zip code, when its winter and they warm your jeans for you before you try them on. My goodness! Did that feel amazing? Good Lawd, we should have invested our money better. But really, warm jeans in the winter.

♦

Steel sharpens steel. Please stop pillow fighting.

♦

The first draft of this book was so confusing and over the top that my copy editor said she didn't want anyone to know she worked on it, if published as is. Stop acting like that, Jina Simmons! You know you had fun debating with me for hours in that cafe on Tompkins Ave. You were giving me that graduate literary discipline and I was stretching the shit out of this thing called Artistic License. I do appreciate you. This book came out waaaay better because of your influence and those debates.
Thank you

♦

Famous quote from Jina, "I just finished another section, I think we can finally move on but I wanted clarity on something first." "Cool, what's that?" "What the hell are you talking about?"

♦

Doctors need doctors. Lawyers need lawyers. Never think one person has all the answers.

♦

My age: When I sported white gold diamond fangs they were still called Fronts. *Grills* weren't introduced yet.

♦

When I parted ways with those fangs and still sported a fangless version, they were still called Fronts.

♦

While in college my freshman year I lost those Fronts. It didn't bother me much because I knew I outgrew that stage in my life.

♦

Someone once said to me, "You are always moving, doing something. You know you could give it a break. That's healthy too. What's the likelihood of you stopping, maybe quitting?" I told them, "You have a better chance of seeing someone sip a milkshake with a coffee straw or seeing Michael Jordan pass the rock in the clutch."

◆

"Chris Rock gaining weight. Bentley making a scooter. Finding a nympho in a platonic relationship. A secret society with open enrollment. Christopher Reeves doing the limbo. A gold digger returning your change." And then they said, "I get it, I get it. Are you done?" "No! A better chance of seeing 54'11s with an air bubble. Flava Flav being taken seriously after *Surreal Life*. Stephen Hawking lip-singing a gospel song. Watching someone scale a vertical wall with vegetable oil on their thumbs. You have a better chance of seeing a unicorn fuck a mermaid with a leprechaun watching." I'll be done with a pillow under my head and/or grit under my nails.

◆

The funny thing is, I never lost those Fronts. Antonia, my girlfriend while in college who was 9 years my senior hid them because she hated the look. I guess my diamond Fronts didn't mesh with her Fendi handbags. She revealed the sabotage after I graduated. Dammit Toni! You saw the maturity, I had at least one more semester to rock out.

◆

Rocking a fresh pair of suede kicks and it starts raining? No worries, we were never too cool for plastic bags. Premature burial avoided. They will live to stunt another day.

◆

The difference between buying goods from a Booster and buying goods from a Crackhead. Boosters had flava options. Crackheads had the complete mystery grab bag. For example, a bag with a pair of designer jeans and a leather jacket verses a bag with a watch, VCR, ladies perfume and a fishing rod. Like I said "Complete Mystery". You could talk down the price to both but there was a major difference in how far. Boosters had deals based on the street market value. Crackhead prices were based on the severity of their withdrawal symptoms. Needless to say, Crackheads had way better price cuts. You just hoped the merchandise was in your size.

♦

Here is a legit question and I only ask because I did not care to google it. Do they still make girl bikes? And if they do, do feminists use them? I mean, when I was young, the top tube coming from the headset to the seat post was parallel to the ground for boys and angled down about 45° for girls. Aside from color, that was the main distinction. If you were a little kid riding a bike that was way too big for you (me being the average height for an 8-year-old trying to ride my father's bike who stood at 6'9), that pole was there to remind you that nut pain is a unique sensation that cannot be replicated with any other injury. From what I heard, getting hit in the pussy sucks too. Still though, boy bikes look cooler. So, ladies, in the spirit of liberation and fashion, let's get rid of those girl bikes, if they still make them and share in this unique, often accidental feeling that can only be understood from experience. Oh wow! It almost sounds like I'm talking about love. Nope, just smashed McNuggets and Puff Pillow agony.

♦

If I were a 1 year old and I couldn't speak: My Thoughts in Jazz
Tip tip... tap tap.... bip bip..... bat bat
Tippy tip.... bitty bat.... slack smack.... kitty kat.....
Rippy rip.... rippity rap.... clickity click....clackity clack...Picky shack....
shackity nip....nippy pack... lacky sips....Sandy landy misty candy....
Dydodee.... deedo dat..... diddy gritty....alley.... ladder daddy. I like waffles....(finger snaps). HA!

◆

The first time my brother Ta and I ever had a heated exchange. I convinced my friend Thomas, who was like 20 years older than me, to let me rock his $7,000 Rolex to school for a week. So, of course I'm stunting in class hard like "This is my out-of-school watch, I usually just rock it on special occasions." My computer teacher thought it was fake at first. Then he examined it. He saw that smooth second hand sweep and thought a 17-year-old with a Submariner is probably a drug dealer. Back to my brother though. During the first day of stunting I came home and Ta and I-Born we're in my room (The recently discovered hang out spot, remember it was living room size.) "Peace G, what's the science?", the usual greeting. We exchanged wisdom. Then, "Yo, Yo, What's that on your wrist?" "It's a Rollie." "You wearing fake shit now?" "Hell to the no, this shit real." "Yeah right, let me see that." I showed them, they examined it, saw that smooth second hand sweep. "Yooo, that shit is real! Let me see that." "See!" "Nah, take it off, we can pawn it and all get some bread." "Hell no. It's my boy's watch." "So, tell him you got robbed." "Hell fucking no. I just told you it's my boy's watch" "You know how much that thing is worth? We definitely pawning that. He can get another one." "No the Fuck we not." "You gonna pick your boy over us?" "What kind of dumb question is that? I'm not picking shit. He let me rock with it and I'm gonna return it." "Ight whatever! I'll be back later, but we definitely pawning that watch." Grimmy was a very popular word used in the 90's. That story was the true definition. My brother always laughs when I remind him of what happened. Thomas still has that Rolex on his wrist today.

◆

Oh, yeah, I like grilled salmon over a bed of rice pilaf, paired with a garden green salad, a splash of balsamic vinaigrette and topped with crumbled blue cheese. Crumbled blue cheese! Who would have known? I'm feeling very adult-ish.

◆

At a certain point, I couldn't stand to see someone with the same pair of kicks as me. Maybe because I didn't have the money to buy a new pair at the same time as the rest of the in crowd. I needed my fresh to last longer. My creativity was in hyper drive. I started to paint, color and dye brand new sneakers just to make sure they were one-off. I was always excited to debut them. If only my friends knew how many times I came to school with colorful damp socks because I was too impatient to wait another day to let my exclusive kicks dry. Scarcity is the mother of innovation.

◆

No thank you, she has too much bottom face. Yup! Just like Travolta. Nah, she has too much side face like a small billboard. Nope, her walk is too busy! Men walk with their shoulders; woman walk with their hips. Any other way confuses my genotype. Prettay Pickay!

♦

Have you ever woken up abruptly from a deep sleep thinking you overslept and then realized that you actually woke up about two hours earlier than your scheduled alarm and then sat there thinking which thought affected you more: The relief from the fact that you were not late for your event or the frustration of knowing that you just fucked up your sleep?

♦

I went through a phase when I hated being in High School. I felt I should be somewhere else. Where? Anywhere but my school. I wanted to transfer. I grew so tired of the high school setting, the curriculum, the teachers, the social aspect. Dean Ragusa brought me back to reality. "You're a junior with good grades. You're even on the Dean's List, stick it out. You came this far. Senior year is right around the corner, then you are outta here." I took heed to his words but in my protest, I decided to take every Monday off for the whole second half of my junior year. That didn't include any other day that I missed during the week for miscellaneous reasons. I was guaranteed absent 1-2 days per week. I even told my teachers which assignments I would not complete beforehand. I told a few teachers, "I will come to class, of course not Mondays. I will participate and take tests but I will not do any homework, labs and/or projects." Most teachers responded like, "The hell you won't. Then I will have no choice but to fail you." I'm like, "It's cool, I understand." The reason I brought this story up was because for the ones who based a heavy percentage of their scores on homework, projects and attendance, I expected a failing grade to be a 60, if that. One teacher, Mrs. Parkinson, the chemistry teacher gave me a 50. Really!!! A fucking 50! I knew I was going to fail her class but that's wrong. I could see a 60, 55 if you don't like the kid, but a 50! She really helped to screw up my average for senior year. Yeah, I know I was screwing it up anyway, but a 50! Mrs. Parkinson didn't like how comfortable I was with letting her fail me. A goddamned 50. I didn't see that coming.

◆

Going to a party was only time you willingly went out, knowing you might ruin your fresh kicks. You just hoped the daylight would be a little more forgiving then your memory, because you damn sure felt every bump and scuff. In the moment, numbers and dubs made up for it. Numbers and Dubs!

◆

Does anyone say "Believe you me" anymore?

◆

During freshman and half of sophomore year, coming home from school, at least twice a week, True and I would be interrogated on the corner of Jefferson ave. and Malcolm X Blvd. by the older guys in the neighborhood. We could've just finished midterm exams or finals. We could've had projects and book reports due. One thing was constant though, the corner convos. "When was the last time y'all got some pussy?" Yup, budding students with the prospects of higher learning and this was the theme. It was either that and/or *shooting the five*. Fight or fucking. This was a rite of passage in most hoods. Making money was a later discussion reserved by age. The saving money discussion, almost nonexistent. The multi-generational wealth discussion—that was alien.

Not to be confused with our parents, who would address those three discussions indoors. This was street culture. Once you stepped outside, this was our reality.

◆

If you break someone's will, you can put anything in its place. Be careful of the substitute.

◆

Values will convince a liberal to wait for a bedroom. Hormones will persuade a conservative to have sex in public. Ahhhh Yes! Public fornication; the *Straight Flush* when sharing stories. Only outdone by the *Royal Flush* of stories; the coveted ménage.

◆

Self-proclaimed photography: Thomas let me hold his high-priced cameras; a big ass Canon 35mm SLR and a small ass Canon Powershot. I immediately snapped pictures of everything and even started charging people ($100 per roll "36 exposures"). In hindsight, I had 2 ½ customers.

I would take turns bringing both cameras to school. One time in particular, I brought the SLR and a unipod to the school cafeteria and told everyone, "We taking a group pic, Come on y'all." About 25-30 kids got up and jumped in the picture. Like, "Oh shit, E taking the ill classic." I snapped about five shots and was done. I knew I caught some good footage. Right after school I went to the Kodak photo shop on Nostrand Ave. Walked in the store with a smile on my face, made it to the register and opened the camera. The compartment was empty. "Ain't that a bitch!" Those types of cameras did not have an indicator mark showing if film was present. So, if you checked it and it was empty, cool. If not, you just ruined the entire roll inside. I didn't want to take the chance and check because I took a ton of pics earlier during that day. That cafeteria shot was the highlight. Fucking Thomas said he loaded it before I picked it up. Fucking old Fuck. All those shots and all I have is this story.

◆

If everyone loved you, you wouldn't know how much someone really loves you. Contrast is the night to your glorious day.

◆

I once had a part time job as a window mannequin in the storefront window of Moshood, an African clothing boutique on Fulton street, downtown Brooklyn. After school, a couple days a week for a few hours I would pose lifeless, changing expressions every several minutes and changing outfits every hour. Shorty-Lo and surprisingly but very true, Flava Flav (nope, I don't know him personally), would pop up (literally) once in a while and make silly faces trying to make me laugh. They were good but I never broke character. Moshood, the owner, liked the way I posed with the other female models, because interested patrons were actually buying those outfits or at least coming in the shop to check out the other fashions. He recognized a young predator and respected my pursuits. Moshood knew that I would find ways to run game with those young ladies while posing. He got a kick out of it and would schedule different models with me. Eventually he would pair me with multiple girls. He would spice it up by having me work with new girls and girls I spoke to already. Almost like a test to see how I would fair. "Young man? You think you can handle three or more ladies?" Rising to the occasion was my middle name. I made those coed group poses classy yet seductive. Do you know how hard it is to flirt and get numbers while being perfectly still? Let's just say, I started that job as mannequin, and ended the job as a ventriloquist.

♦

But even more impressive, do you know how hard it was for a 15yr old to grab a woman's waist or have her super soft plump derriere pressed against his body and not get a *hard on*. Man I tell you, I passed that test but I should've been paid more for exhibiting such restraint.

♦

For any girl who wears granny panties on a date and decides to become intimate on that engagement: keep in mind that when your date looks at those parachute drapes, it reminds him of an adult wearing diapers. It probably won't stop most guys from
indulging, but come on ladies! Save it for your cycle and let's make this world a sexier place......HA!

♦

I know what you may be thinking, "How rude! Those Granny Panties are comfortable" and you might be right but so are orthopedic shoes yet you don't see those shits on the runway. DOUBLE HA!

♦

No offense to senior citizens who pair their panties with orthopedic shoes. Some dude with a cane thinks you are hot shit! I'LL MINUS ONE HA!

♦

When I was 14 years old I tried to get the number of a woman in her mid 20's. She said, "Awww, look at you, you're cute. It will be like robbing the cradle. See me when you get older. Your money is too short anyway." Two things, 1. Straight rejection. 2. I had no idea, at first, what she was talking about. "Money" I thought we did this for fun. She must have been a professional. Hahahahaha

♦

High school prom: Everything had to be extra. I initially wanted to be accompanied by several dates. I also wanted to arrive on a motorcycle (which at the time, I hadn't ever personally ridden one) and not unless my dates were riding motorcycles too, those logistics weren't looking too good. I changed the game plan. I didn't like the idea of a limousine, so I rented a hunter green BMW 325i. Most students weren't driving, let alone a Bimmer, so I was naturally feeling myself. I have to thank Thomas again. I paid cash and the rental went under his name. I also needed some custom wear. My sister, U-U, who was a designer at the time, made me a pair of aqua blue snakeskin leather pants and an aqua blue and black snakeskin leather and crushed silk tank top. (For the record, snakeskin leather later came in style like two seasons later and got played out fast because of the fashion world's tacky application of it. So, if you see those prom pictures, remember, don't judge me. Ha.) I asked Majida who was 24 years old at the time to be my date. My sister made her a hot pink and aqua snakeskin leather short dress. Majida was the best player when it came to prom night stunting. She cut off all her hair and rocked a caesar for the occasion. It was past shoulder length before the cut. Oh, and she dyed her hair hot pink to match the dress. I was super feeling myself. Prada's from Barney's from the half off gift card hook up (everybody knew somebody) and a pair of space-aged Chanel shades. It would have been Gucci but somebody's Rottweiler ate them shits the week before. Yeah, Thomas again trying to be cool. Feed them damn dogs!

I already had a gold Movado watch and diamond fronts. I just needed the gold Byzantine chain with the iced-out fish piece from Ta, the flooded diamond bracelet from I.G., and the blinged out pinky ring from Born Preme. "You better not get robbed." "Ain't nobody gonna try to rob me." "Nigga, with all that shit on, if I didn't know you, I would try to rob you." I did listen to some of the advice though, "Don't stop too long at a corner, even if it's red light. After a few seconds, run that shit. Don't give anybody time to scheme on you." Once we arrived, the faculty was like "Who the fuck!" Majida and I spent more time taking pictures then dancing. Aside from the paparazzi party, she stayed low key and watched me rock out like Rick James. That was one hell of a night.

♦

When prom night ended, I still had to drop Majida back home in Flatbush, take the Bimmer back to Thomas in Harlem, just to take the A-Train back to Bed-Stuy, shower, change. Then turn a 17-minute walk into 8 minutes to get back to school in order to the catch the 8am charter bus to go on our senior trip to Six Flags Great Adventure. And I forgot to put deodorant on before that sprint walk. Had me questioning myself that whole damn bus ride. That was one hell of a morning.

♦

I would NEVER be caught holding hands during that period in my life.

It carried such a sappy connotation; ironically I didn't mind an arm lock.

♦

It is often said that the eyes are the window to the soul. I agree. I would like to add to that. Your skin is the window to your health and your mouth is the window to your brain. Which means if you pay attention, in a matter of minutes, even seconds, someone will reveal their character, health and intellect all at the same time. But you don't hear me though.

♦

My father attended my high school graduation downtown at the Marriott. He watched the class valedictorian give her speech. He saw various students receiving all sorts of awards and honors. When I received my diploma, he looked at me and said, "What happened to the others. Why didn't you receive any awards?" I replied, "I didn't know you wanted them."

♦

He passed away during my sophomore year at college. I graduated with honors and a host of accolades. The irony.

♦

Rev. Al Sharpton was the keynote speaker at my high school graduation. I don't remember the speech but at the time we all felt he did a great job. Before it was time to walk to the podium and receive my diploma, my brother Ta handed me a three-foot tall champagne glass. When my name was called and I made my way to the stage, Mr. Mickens (the principal) shook my hand, looked at me and smiled, looked at the glass and started shaking his head. I raised that glass high in the air to honor my peers. I don't even like champagne.

♦

I also borrowed this girl's Acura, whom I just met less than a week ago, to drive my grandmother and some family members to that same graduation. That was the second time I drove with a license. Such a good look! I can remember my older brother Ski now, "What! One of your girls has a car. Everyone can't fit in my whip. You better get that car and stop playing and drive your mother and grandmother. I don't even know her but I know she'll give it to you." He was right. I really wish I could remember her name but I'm sure it's in that little black book. She was an unsung hero.

♦

To everyone from my high school (Boys and Girls High School b.k.a. THE HIGH) who has risen above the status quo and who has invested time and money in themselves, I salute you. I support you all. Even if your t-shirts do cost $100 dollars. I would buy shoe laces if you sold them. And to all other high schoolers, support your peers, we are the world's future leaders and followers.

♦

"**What are you doing next weekend?**" "I'm not sure yet." "You want to hang out? Maybe go somewhere?" "I would love to, but I don't want to commit to that time just yet. If something comes up; the studio, work or a shoot, I would have to cancel. And I don't wanna leave you hanging. I respect your time." "It's like I need advanced bookings with you. I understand you are busy and all and you have a lot going on and I get that, but if you truly wanted to see someone, like really wanted to be with them, it doesn't matter what is happening in your life, you will find a way to make time for them." I sat there in awkward silence, thinking does she know *Logic*? Because IF what she said is true THEN this has to be one of the dumbest conversations we are having.

◆

"Hey, how you been?" "I'm good, the family is good, everybody getting big" "Do you know who you are talking too?" "Of course I do" "Who then?" "Now you want to insult my intelligence" "Who?" "Trust me I know; your voice isn't that common. Anyway, what's happening? You going out this weekend?" Five minutes into the conversation, Oh shit! This isn't Abigail. It was an honest mistake, sometimes we thought we knew.

◆

The first time I ever got jumped, True and I were coming home from playing basketball. We were serving them, giving them the business, on their turf. Clapping the backboard on a lay-up was the next best thing to dunking. Of course, we won. But during free play somebody got hit smack dead on the head by an air ball thrown from half court. They thought we did it. We didn't. But winning and laughing wasn't so convincing. So, we had a 5 on 2 brawl at the end of the night. Thomas and Lloyd are the only names I remember. This was the first time somebody tried to play us. Emotions were high. When asked by our brothers and the older guys on the block how we would like to handle it,

"They gotta go, either everyone dies or we get the one on one." That was a real response. Our brothers and the older guys, "Nah, y'all can't do 'em like that. Yall can scrap though. Maybe buss 'em in the head with something if you want." We ran through their area several times to no avail. We couldn't catch them on the block, couldn't even find them on the courts. The streets were dead. I found out Lloyd went to The High. He didn't know I was a student there. This was 9th grade. I walked the halls for three weeks with a pencil in my hand ready to stab him in the face on sight. Being played on the street for the first time can do that to you. We never crossed paths in the hallway. We never saw him after school. Time passed, we didn't forgive or forget, we just accepted it. Finally, a home address and schedule were revealed, but at that time we matured already. How does this tie into my high school sneaker pimp ways you might ask? I was talking to his sister.

♦

I traded my Red Satin Polo Ball Varsity jacket with Jay for a wool Armani sweater and some Lo button ups. That sweater was itchy as fuck. Damn you Jay!

♦

It's funny how one day dry humping was so natural it was expected. Then as we got older, it was like, what the hell is this? Are we fucking or what?

♦

You are only a cheater if you keep secrets. Where's my bullhorn?

♦

Super random. Upstairs from my apartment, I'm at a get-together. This was years after high school, a few years after college to be exact. I'm working the crowd in my usual Doctor Octopus ways. (I might explain later, but if you read the book it will make sense.) As I'm conversing with a group, one girl in particular said, "I remember you." I was drawing a blank. "Really, from where?" "We met in front of a school building. You approached me while I was with my mother. We both thought it was bold but you were polite, so I gave you my number."

Sounds like something I would do but I was still drawing a blank. "When we spoke on the phone, you asked me to be your prom date. You told me, I would be one of three. I didn't agree and I don't think we ever spoke after that." I couldn't stop laughing for two reasons: 1. I vaguely remembered her and 2. I knew she was telling the truth because that sounded like some shit I would say. Her friends shook their heads in disbelief. I was still laughing. I told her I'm finishing up a book about experiences like the one she mentioned. "I still have my little black book as a reference for when the book comes out. If you gave me your number, it would definitely be in there." I left the party, went back down to the apartment and retrieved the book from an old shoe box. There she was, Candice. The 261st entry, with a description that read "In front of B&G with mother" with a line crossed through the name. I told you that prom thing was so extra.

♦

Sneaker pimp first. I'm not gonna talk about things I had first, that's pretty lame…. But I was the first one in my school with a beeper watch. Most likely the first and only. I'm sure of that. You know how I know I'm sure, because if you are reading this, you just learned that beeper watches were even out in the mid 90's.

♦

What's better than a card trick? Undoing a bra with one hand. That's the closest we ever came to becoming magicians.

♦

Shorty-Lo and his mother's car: Ok, I'll try to keep this short. Shorty-Lo and his family moved from the Stuy to Canarsie. He was bored as Fuck, always tryna get me to take that long ass trip on the L train and what felt like an even longer trip walking to his house from that train. He would bait me by saying he has girls coming through. (He wasn't lying but sometimes things didn't go as planned.) Many times, we would end up cutting girls off (crossing a line through their name and number so that we would never call them again) just because they didn't want to take the trip to meet us. I was somewhat empathetic to their position because I didn't want to make that trip either.

"Aight, I'm not doing this shit anymore. This was a bust. Now I have this long ass trip back home." "Nah, I got you. I'll take you back." "How?" "Let's wait till my mom falls asleep, then I'll get her minivan and drive you back." "Bet!" This became the routine. One particular time I was like "Nah, B. Not today. I know you got me on the way back but I don't even feel like jumping on the train to get there." "It's cool, you don't have to because I'll be in the Stuy later. I'll scoop you and bring you back home." "I know it must be boring as shit out there. Aight I'm with it."

On the way to Canarsie, using our black books of course, I asked him, "You ever got caught taking your mom's car?" "Nah, never." "When do you put gas in it?" "I don't put gas in this joint." "What? you telling me you been taking her car like twice, three times a week and you never put back the gas you used?" "Nope!" "And she doesn't notice?" "Nah". At this point we were about to approach an intersection. Shorty-Lo asked me, "Yo E, should I take this turn super-fast or super slow." "Super fast" "Yoouuuu got it." This had to be the funniest slash scariest car scene of that time. Shorty-Lo mashes the pedal and makes a right off of Halsey street. Not sure he realized how fast we were going or how fast he turned the wheel. I'm actually pretty laid back while this is happening. My father and all of my brothers drove fast when I was coming up, so I was a bit used to it. Back to Shorty-Lo. We just missed an oncoming car and he definitely over turned that steering wheel because now we were about to run up on the sidewalk. "OH SHIT!" He yanks the wheel back the opposite way just in time for us not to jump the curb. The front passenger wheel smacks the lip of the sidewalk. "OHHHH SHIT!!" "FUCK!" a couple more yards and he stops the car.

We get out. He needs to breathe for a few seconds to regain his composure. "Damn son, you wilin'." "I know, that shit was crazy." Next, we walked around the car to assess the situation. We thought it was much worse than it was - still not good though. "You lucky as shit. That sidewalk is dumb high. I thought the whole front bumper was done." "I know. Me too." "That hubcap rim is scraped the fuck up though. Your moms gonna flip!" "Damn. Fuck! Nah we good. She won't notice it." "What! You's a funny guy. How the hell wouldn't she notice that?" "Nah, we definitely good, I'm telling you. Let's just drive regular. If the cops were here we really would have been fucked. I don't have a license." "Yeah, me neither."

Fast forward to the next week. "Yooo, Big E from the Stuy." "Wuts goodie?" "I have a girl for you. And she loves dudes with dreads. I already set it up. You good money." "Ok, ok, now we talking." "But you have to come out here and I can't drive you back either." "Really? what happened?" "Mom dukes found out I was taking the car." "I knew it. I told ya ass. Ain't no way in hell you drive every day and won't notice a half tank of gas missing." "Yea, I'm sorta on punishment. She noticed the gas missing for weeks and was just waiting. She said she was seeing if I was gonna fill it back up. She also noticed that big ass gash on that hubcap rim"

♦

I ran for student body president in high school and in college. I used the same picture in both campaigns. I lost twice. It was a set up I tell ya.

♦

The indentation format for chapter 7 and the end chapter 5 was deliberate.

♦

Speaking of chapter 7, I bet you didn't see that shit coming. That steam was intentionally added for the ladies. Owww!

♦

X-rated nostalgia: Every game of *Truth or Dare* ended up being sexual. I thought that was the whole point of playing the game.

♦

For all of the wildness of the 90's we were still well mannered. 'Airing it out' was a different clique. Not active but always ready. Every day I carried a knife, box cutter, a scalpel (when your neighbor is a RN). I even had a retractable police baton, slash resistant Kevlar gloves, and some spiked knuckled gloves (I have no idea where I got my spiked gloves from.) All those blades and never had to use them, never even flashed them. For the few fist fights I had, my life was never in danger. He was close to getting that pencil though. I was told once you draw, finish the picture.

♦

The truth shall set you free. No, really! If you are too blunt, too soon, your date may end early, setting you free to do other things. The truth in the beginning of a relationship is time sensitive. I won't be too direct with my intentions and she won't be too open with her feelings. Nothing worse than trying to fuck someone who wants to get married. Or trying to marry someone who wants to get fucked. Let's get it together people.

♦

Shorty-Lo and I were famous for going to girls houses to chill and get our grub on. This could have been a girl of interest or just a platonic friend of either one of us. Funny but true. And if they had an older sister or young mother, he would warn them, "I bet you five dollars E try to talk to your moms." "Yeah right." The moment we walked in, we greeted the family. "Peace, Peace, Peace. Yall cooked already? Any snacks? Anything? You got milk in the fridge? Cereal works." "So you just gonna refuse to age? Man, I tell you, if I was just a few weeks older. Me and you, like nobody's business."

♦

Many think they are artists, only to find out they have been tracing the whole time. It's never too late to pick up a brush.

♦

Hey ladies, you want to know how to naturally throw off his circadian rhythm? At the very last minute, cancel a late night booty call. I mean really last minute; like after he performed the mad dash clean-up of his place and put on some smell goods. Like after you already confirmed your arrival time and he is just calculating how long the cab ride will be, while he patiently waits there in his figurative silk robe.

♦

Hey ladies, you want to know if he really likes you past his sexual desires? See if you get a phone call during the daytime after that last minute booty call cancellation.

♦

Ron handed me my first pistol while at a party. It was the age of Aquarius. He gave me a Taurus. The place was packed with girls. It was packed with strangers too. Needless to say, I couldn't get my dub on. Wait a second, why is it that nobody in the hood had holsters? I really would like a legit answer. If you can buy illegal guns, you can definitely buy legal holsters. I can't get jiggy with this shit.

♦

Sneaker Pimp Chronicles: The early years. Mark got locked up. Knowing that he would be gone for a while, he decided to give me damn near all of his kicks. All fresh. 85% were still new in the box. I had more

Fila's then I knew what to do with. That was over 12 pairs for a 12yr old. After that, options were a must. My sneaker Pimpdom was born.

♦

Talking with your hands can be very effective when expressing yourself. The listener has a chance to feel your energy and see your words. Talking with your hands while on the phone. Well, that's just weird. Calm down please.

♦

A spring night, in the back of a Jeep Wrangler with my godfather, Billy and his boy, Vlad. The temperature was cool enough to wear jackets but we still had the top off. I'm 13 years old. We pulled up to a light, I noticed a young girl in the car next to us. I ask her to roll down her window. Straight to the point, "You are beautiful, What's your name? Your number?" The light turns green. She shouts her name and her number from the back window of that car. "Who has a pen?" We scramble, Vlad has to pull off because of traffic. Billy yells, "No pen!" Both cars moving and I yell to her car, "Say it again." She does one last time, right before her car has to turn in the opposite direction. "Did she say 5 or 9?" The guys laugh at the whole scene. One of the reasons why bringing me along with them was so easy. I didn't drink, I didn't smoke. I couldn't even relate to adult issues. But girls, that was a common denominator. I was definitely more than a digit off because I never figured out that number.

♦

Is it me or is YKK the Rupert Murdoch of zippers. Really! Is there any legit competitor for that company? If you don't believe me, look at your crotch.

♦

The Last Shorty-Lo story. There are way too many but this is the last cameo he gets in my book. That's it for you buddy! Washington Irving night school, this is what happens when idle time meets a lack of diverse after-school programs meets creative teens. "Yo, Big E from da Stuy." "What's up brother?" "I know where we can bag a slew of chicks and play basketball at the same time" "Where?" "Washington Irving High School. Night school. Its downtown Manhattan off of 14th street." "What? I'm not posting up in front of no school waiting for girls and taking a train to get there? You bugging." "Nah, I ain't doing that shit either.

Listen to me. Night school is for kids who need make up credits for their regular daytime school. We enroll in night school with fake names and just pick gym classes. Go there, talk to girls, play B-ball and then go home. That's twice a week straight fun and bitches. We just have to get a guidance counselor to sign off with a letter saying we need extra credits." "Hmmm, Mrs. Smith (RIP) is dumb cool with me. We can try her." "That's what I'm talking about. You'll see, Watch! You'll thank me, I passed by there the other night, it's mad girls in that school." Mrs. Smith was very chill though, and we had a mutual line of respect, so I kept it funky with her. "Mrs. Smith, you have a second?" "Sure, Akasa." "It's Eternal" "Did your mama name you Eternal? I'm just messin' with you. What's up E? What can I do for you?"

"Long story short, there aren't much things to do after school, not even a nearby gym to go to. Andy and I wanted to sign up for night school at Washington Irving High School just to go to gym, maybe talk to some young ladies but mostly gym. We aren't the stand on the corner type of guys. It's for students who need the make-up credits so we need a guidance counselor from here to sign this form saying we need the credits. It won't get back to you. We're not gonna use our real names." Don't think about any other holes in that dialogue. Just know that it happened. That was a real conversation, and she actually signed those papers (back then ID's were paper passes with no pictures). "Yo E, you the man. You know Norman Thomas High School has night classes too." "My brotha! Chill, let's just rock out with this. I'm not pressed for girls like that." I really wish I could remember the name that Shorty-Lo used because some people actually commented like "Matthew? Corey!? You guys don't look a Matthew and Corey." "And you don't look like whatever the fuck your name is either." That whole situation was hysterical.

The day we went to Washington Irving to register for classes, we were told that we can't sign up for double gym. And that two classes were mandatory for registration. So, that meant gym and a real class. "This some bullshit. You said we can take gym back to back." "I thought we could. Don't worry. Let's just choose an easy class that probably has more girls in it. You not doing the work anyway, Corey! Let them fail Corey. It will be on Corey's record. Just make sure you pick gym or P.E. as the second class." "Aight, whatever!"

And there it was, twice a week we took Spanish and Gym. Playing basketball, flirting, bagging, and talking shit. He was right, there were a ton of girls there from different neighborhoods, all with different attitudes and personalities. The gym class was flooded. Most girls failed gym because they didn't get dressed, not because of participation. So, in this class all the girls got dressed and then sat down on the side. Shorty-Lo and I were playing super extra, like it was *Soul in the Hole* (A Brooklyn basketball tournament) meets *Harlem Globetrotters*, trying to shoot 3-pointers and dunk on every possession (we had an audience).

The ratio must have been a known thing because when school let out, cars would be parked outside lined up. Dudes where straight stunting trying to holla at the surplus. LB even showed up with a full-length fur. Fun times. We actually made some good friends from that gym class. Shaunte was the closest I came to being boo'd up in my whole high school experience and she wasn't even from my school. Our Spanish classmates liked us too. Even the teacher was concerned about our progress. That's because even though we never did her homework, we participated with enthusiasm. "You guys are awesome. I love the energy you bring to the class but I'm a little concerned. Without the homework, you will need about a perfect score on the final exam to pass this class."

"This class is awesome Mr. Rosa (???). Don't worry, we've been studying and preparing really hard." Yea, preparing really hard not to be in class come test time! Can't take away the memories. We actually tried to sign up the following term but somehow the gym teacher found out we had fakes name. He reported us to the administrators. They banned us from ever returning to Washington Irving.

◆

Speaking of Shaunte. I remember the first time she came to Bed-Stuy to check me. She actually did have on a polo-style shirt that was just long enough to be a skirt (very nice). I had on a blue denim colored Coogi. I'll spare you the details of what went down. It was the after event that made this story worth telling. When she was ready to leave I already knew I was walking her to the train. It was sunny. She was gorgeous, fly as shit and I liked her. If I wasn't feeling her I would have never made it past the vestibule of my house. Anyway, as we are walking, joking, laughing, smiling, I told her that I will wait for her train to come before I leave the station. In my head, I'm like "Yeah E, you are some kind of wonderful. She definitely deserves the walk to the train but you are going to actually wait for the train to come. And they said chivalry was dead." Her response caught me off guard. "So when I get on the train how would you know I got home safe?" "Ummm, you would call me when you got home." I replied like it was common date knowledge. "That leaves a lot to chance. I came all the way to see you in Brooklyn and you are not going to take me back home? I never come to Brooklyn EVER. I have family in Brooklyn, somewhere and I haven't even visited them."

Hold up, hold up, what was happening here? In that day and age, no one was expecting a cab ride between boroughs, especially not in the daytime. We were clearly walking to the train station. What did she mean by take her back? Ohhhhhhh, she meant get on the train with her, go back to Manhattan, and then get back on the train and come home. What in the blue blazes was that about? "Really? I'm gonna be on the train all day doing that." "You're a guy. You'll be ok. Would you want me on the train by myself looking like I'm just wandering around?" Alright, so we negotiated that one a little. I did take the train with her back to midtown but I never left the station. I told her, "Ok, if you don't make it home from the station to your house, then this whole world is fucked." She laughed, gave a parting hug, a little tongue action and then she said, "Call me when you get home, so I know you made it back safe." "Doesn't that leave a lot to chance?" I replied. "You're a guy!" Some double standards were acceptable.

◆

"This was the best dish I have ever had. Oh by the way, I don't cook often and I've only been to two restaurants." -- When confident influencers don't have enough experience.

◆

If you've never cleaned your laces, this sneaker pimping wasn't for you.

◆

If you collected sneakers and didn't understand why some people kept, white shoe polish, dish detergent and tooth brushes handy then you are probably a second-generation sneaker pimp.

◆

In most cultures, people wear sneakers to play around in and use dress shoes to go formal. In my culture, we wear sneakers to play around in and better sneakers to dress up with.

◆

My first house party and the first and only time my mother ever caught me (Remember that police precinct): Before I get to the "caught part". Earlier that week, I threw my first party at my cousin Malcolm's loft in Park Slope. Don't smile for me yet. It wasn't the row of one and two family brownstones, trendy eateries and boutiques part of Park Slope. This place was in the industrial, you need to take two trains, then walk 10 blocks just to get to a building that looked like the mob used it for drop-offs part of Park Slope.

Ironically enough, Malcolm did eventually get a duplex later in that trendy area I first mentioned, where I would occasional house sit. Let me pause for a second and appreciate my cousin Malcolm. Over the course of high school, he let me house sit 4-5 times at different locations (a loft, a condo, and two brownstones). He only had one rule, "I don't mind you having company. Just don't FUCK IN MY BED." "Fair enough." Let's fast forward to how my mother caught me later that week. Directions to that mafia loft location proved to be problematic for most girls, so I ended up having more guys in attendance at my party. Music was dope, lights and space were great, but that ratio was terrible. I mean, there was enough guys to play a scrimmage game in any sport kind of terrible, so I called an audible. Never forgetting the play that counts. "Let's shut this thing down, but not before I step to those two over there".

Later that week, I convinced "Those two" to come through to my house. "Bring your homegirl, I have a guy for her". I called up Ade (Ah-Day) and told him it was going down. "When? where?" was his reply. Those should be the only questions from a team player.

Fast Forward even more to later that night. My dancehall mix was hitting crazy, Mr. Vegas and Capleton going hard in the background. I'm on one side of the room with my date. Ade is on the other with his. Things already transpired. Ade and I had put our clothes back on. The girls only half, from the top up. That's only because at the end we were playing a wild game with ice cubes. They had to wait or leave with wet pants. (We didn't want anyone to catch a cold. We were gentlemen and it was winter for Christ sake.) It was a little after 3am. My door creaked open. My mother walks in. "What the hell is going on here?" "Hey Ma." "Hey Mama-Leela." "Ade." "Hello." "Young lady! Where are your pants?!?!" "Ma, I wasn't doing anything. Look, I have my pants on. I can't be doing anything if my pants are on." "Young lady, put back on your pants, the both of you!" "Yes Ma'am." "Mama-Leela, I have some pants on too." "Yes I see that, Ade. I was upstairs sleeping and I heard noise or some music and I'm thinking who is even up at this blasted hour?"

I looked at Ade, "I told you that shit was too loud". It really wasn't but at 3am everything is too loud. The girls rushed to find their pants and then quickly dressed. Not sure what to expect next, we were all caught off guard by my mother's reaction. "Ok, well then, I'm about to make some tea, do you girls want any?" "No ma'am," they said in unison. The four of us in sync shared the same awkward facial expression. I turned to Ade, "That should have been way worse."

♦

Side note: My brother Ta, got caught a few times. He probably could have avoided it if he put back on his pants really quick, my defense attorney advised me. HA

♦

Have you ever felt so tired, relaxed and/or lazy that you thought it required too much energy to focus your eyes? So, you let them cross. Then realized that you were in public and someone might get the wrong idea?

♦

Saying "My Dick" at the end of any statement was actually a punchline, even for girls. Right before "Deez Nutz" came out.

♦

There are some wonderful, acceptable excuses on why you can't make it somewhere. Like, you knocked out early or you were doing something for your mother or you had the dates mixed up on your calendar or even the screwed-up weekend train service schedule. But after conducting a survey with myself, by far the absolute best excuse is…. Dunt Dunna Dah, "You were in the Studio!" Why is this so believable? Because we all know or heard of someone who travels to a studio, this is a real place.

Also, everyone knows that studios are notorious for taking up more time than anticipated. They close when the work is done or people are too tired to be productive. They also know the studio is where magic happens, and who really wants to be the asshole that cock blocks magic? And this isn't just for the musically inclined. You can use any studio activity as an excuse: A dance studio, an art studio. You even could say studio apartment if you talk fast.

♦

My last house party: So, we all just graduated. Well, most of us. On the horizon, a hot summer and the potential for shenanigans. College was a couple months away, so it only made sense to throw a going away party. I learned some valuable lessons from the last party. This time it's at a house, my house, which is close to the school, so travel shouldn't be an issue. Two weeks before the party I invited every girl I knew. You know how girls need to plan shit out. I had to fix that last ratio issue. I invited a few of the homies the day before. You know how guys don't plan shit out. My cousin Otuno as the DJ, Ta doing security. (Ta assumed I would only invite girls so he never planned to check people, someone just needed to be at the door.) My cousins, Mek and Ron in the crowd with them pokers. That's how we always traveled when we went to those Flatbush and Brownsville death trap parties. Not that they even thought we needed to use them. After all, we were in my house. My mother and two of my sisters were downstairs with the food and drinks. A Slim goodie with those Johnny Mellon Camps (big ass titties) literally on my bed. She was home-grown sweetness. She would have been considered a Georgia peach if she was from Georgia. I been rapping to her on the phone for the past several weeks. She didn't even live in NYC. "If I come to your party, where am I going to stay afterwards?" "By me of course. I wouldn't let you jump on a bus that late." Food was smelling delicious. Tunes were banging. The crowd was flowing in. Things were looking really good until I noticed something. "Who the fuck are these people?"

No, really? I invited girls, told them to bring a friend. I only invited a few of my dudes super last minute - many the day of. The one thing that hadn't occurred to me when inviting all those girls, was that THEY would invite other girls and THOSE girls would invite their GUY friends. Those GUYS would tell their GUY friends and eventually the whole neighborhood would know some dude is having a house party with tons of girls. Didn't see that coming. "Yoo E, he cool?" Ta shouted. "Fuck it, it's a party. He cool." "Aight, you good, bathroom, food and shit downstairs."

At that point I didn't mind. I was too busy having fun to care; entertaining company in my room, running through the party laughing with my friends and dubbing with any girl with rhythm. Slim goodie wasn't really a party girl so she stayed in my room most of the night. "That's cool, I'll be back. You hungry?" After about forty minutes of being "the hostess with the mostess", I realized that everyone wasn't smiling. Spydee senses started tingling. I went to see Ta, his Spydee senses were already on it. In my 'Love for Everybody' moment we realized that EVERYBODY was in my house.

Bloods flagged up. Crips flagged up. Random enemies and rivals all showed up looking for a good time and a little get back on a Saturday night. Once things started to look like people were actually scheming on each other, Ta went to the door to address the new arrivals and the ones still in the hallway. I'm on the side, Mek and Ron are in the cut. Ta placed a sawed off with the pistol grip behind the door, "This is my house. Respect my house. My mother lives here. My brother letting you muthafuckas in here. Ain't shit happening here. I don't give a fuck who you are and who you don't like. If it's like that, take it outside. Outside and down the block. I'll let y'all in but if anything happens, I FUCKING promise you, this door closes and nobody going home!

Ta, spit flying off of every sentence, was effective and there was a temporary truce. Ok back to flirting and dubbing. The night was great. I ending up smashing something in the bathroom before entertaining the company in my own room. That's called a Twofer! Eventually everyone cleared out, without incident. Well, not in or in front of the house anyway. Shots did ring out at the corner. The uninvited guests kept their word. That next morning was euphoric. I walked around the house to clean up any leftover garbage. I did a glance over to assess any damages. Surprisingly, Nothing! That many people and the place was still good.

Ohh, there was one thing. The room on the 2nd floor, where we moved all the furniture and used as the dance floor. Well, the walls were smothered in a blue haze. I mean in a complete circle around the room, minus where the DJ booth was, all at waist level. It was the dye from denim jeans, from everyone dancing on the walls, including myself. My mother let me go to college without ever repainting that room.

♦

What ever happened to Jiggy Lisa? She was cool as shit! Definitely a Sneaker Pimp.

♦

As an adult, I never got a chance to thank Mr. Butcher from 10th grade. He saw something unique in me as well as two of my close friends. Out of his own pocket he paid for Rello, Divine (Shorty-Lo) and me to attend acting classes on the weekend, Henry Street Settlement in L.E.S. Those acting students never seen kids like us before. Straight from the inner city, three different personalities; cocky, cool and clowning (not in that order). Of course, we tried to bag every girl with a fatty, but for all the laughs though, we actually performed for those assignments. Dope experience during. Great experience in retrospect.

◆

Ok, this one really dates me. It will be reminiscent for some and history for others. Not too many kids had cell phones in high school, but many of us had beepers/pagers. 9-1-7 is an OG area code. These numerical pagers gave us only one option (yes, one is not an option but that's how people talk); display a return number on the screen of who you were paging. We soon learned how to encrypt words through the numbers. That means, quick and functional; simple return number so they can call you back or simple word encryption. But that wasn't enough for me.

I had to have an alpha-numeric pager, this way you can actually leave a real message on the screen and not this encryption crap, it also stopped you/me from using a pay phone if the message didn't warrant a call back. It even came with updated news stories and stock market updates. Now, how is this story interesting or even funny? Glad you asked. The technology was still fairly new. This was before 2-Way pagers. This particular alpha-numeric pager came with two numbers; the customary 917 number that everyone was used to (where you can only show a return number) and an 1-800 number, that you would give out to people so they can leave you a worded message. Let me pause for a second, you need to understand how cool it was to have two numbers in high school, neither one being your landline—and having one be a 1-800 number. Shit! you only saw 1-800 numbers on TV commercials. Now, I was super sneaker pimping.

Ok, unpause. Where was I? Yea I remember. New technology. No 2-Way pagers. So when someone wanted to leave you a worded message, you gave them the exclusive 1-800 number. They then had to call a live operator and tell them the message, then the operator had to type said-message and send it to your pager. As long as you didn't give the operator any profanity to type, they had to write whatever you said in that message. WHAT-EVER you said. If the girl you were talking to was super cool or freaky, she would turn those operators to soft porn receptionists. Message from: 718-346-xxxx. 4:32pm "Can you cum by later and pound me out please. I'm feeling gushy and I'm ready to ride pipe." Hahahaha, those were the days.

♦

Shaka Zulu, Arnold Schwarzenegger, Bruce Lee, Bruce Leroy.

♦

A Predominantly Black school and there was a phase where we actually wore Nascar jackets. TIDE, M&Ms. DuPont. I had the KODAK. Fashion knew no boundaries.

♦

Lynrich and Skyler, B&G high school dancehall kings. If you ever wanted to see the *bruk up*, all you needed was a hammer fist and a hard surface.

♦

At the age of 9, Ta would bring me along with him to BMCC (Borough of Manhattan Community College) to bag girls for him and his friends. They would post up in the front of the building, see a girl they liked, tell me what to say and usher me off. "Excuse me Miss, my friend in the blue Yankees hat thinks you are the most beautiful girl he has ever seen. He is pretty shy but wanted me to ask for your number or can you wait for a second so that he can come talk with you." "Awww, tell him to come here." In hindsight, for the amount of times we went, and the one time we were actually in the building, it's safe to say they were cutting class. That's also the around the same time the sister of a girl he was talking to open mouth kissed me. She was 20.

♦

Fresh was a must. We put everything in the cleaners, even those t-shirts. Anything else was considered play clothes.

♦

Try something new, converse with someone unlike like yourself, travel somewhere you haven't been before, listen to noise, embrace a new art. You don't have to do it all, just one will have a profound effect. I promise you, it will change how you see the world...but be careful, there is a big difference between being open and being turned out.

♦

The old block, Jefferson Ave. and the neighborhood. If I misspelled your name, or forgot it, you already know what it is. Love is love. Ski, Tamu, O, Deshawn-Divine, Big Tim, Killer Shawn-Killz, Black Shawn, Shawn Lo, U-U, Big Nik, Beezo, Deezo, The Twins, Butter, Dino, Face (RIP), Penny, Shakeema, Troy (RIP), Anthony (RIP) and BoBo, Terron-True, Kasa-Eternal, Antwoine- I-Divine, Wayman (RIP), Ms. Robinson, Pam, Beverly (RIP), Ms.Val (RIP), Peanut, Jarvis, Keith, Jiggy Jay, Kenny Ken man, Milton, Gary (RIP), Dre, Tiny, Frances, Mellow, Ricky,

Mark, Shane, Erving, John John, Kelly, Sam, Dorothy, Micky, Sylvia, Relly, Cynthia, Sandra, Bobby, Nicole, young Danny, I-God, I-Cee, Kevin, Fritz, Shaunte, older Danny, Amaala and Naloge, Randy (RIP), Keith, Mr. and Mrs. Balance, Nancy, Frank, Rodney. Mashwan, Andre, Asia, Born, Amentet, Chad, Sha-Mecca, ReRe, Mrs. Freeman, Mr. Reid, Tuwon-Hook, Tameeka, Marty, Martha, Shy, Nic, Porsche, Mr. Chester, Jahmilia, Old lady Jamila, Jimmy, Yvette, Colin, Petey, Melissa, Jason, Toya, Robin, Ben, Flex, Kisha, Omar, Martha, Ms. Buddy (RIP), Desire, The 680 building, Asia, Mr. Grey, Jerome-Rylo, Dwayne-Math, Tony-Knowledge, Tehran, I-Self, Born Preme, Lil Lei Lei, JJ, Diddy, Gino, Jetta-Lo, Clyneekwa, Tay, Erica, Angie, Candice, Elliot, Tony, Weldon, Travis, Ricky, Ron, Mek, Otanu, Adenibe, Ms. Sherrod, Uncle Terry, Mo-Chips, Mike, Moosh. YOOOOOO! My memory is scary.

◆

You are who you are, when no one is there.

◆

Thank you all for visiting my mindful youth. I mean my youthful mind. This memoir tackled one aspect of life in high school. As students, we had so much going on. Think of it as *first period* in a day full of classes. I hope I made you laugh, smile or even cringe. See you at *second period*, at the entrance to the next book that I will never write, titled:

'You Can't Teach a Horse to fish. The College Years'

Thank you. Thank you all and good night.

Credits

GOD BODY ♦ SEGA BEFORE SEGA GENESIS ♦ FUN DIP ♦ NERDS ♦ LUCKY STRIKE CIGARETTE GUM ♦ L.A. TECS WITH THE REMOVABLE LIGHT ♦ EEK THE CAT ♦ MING FROM FLASH GORDON ♦ HACKSAW JIM DUGGAN ♦ GIGAPETS ♦ EXCITE BIKE ♦ USED JEANS ♦ DAMAGE JEANS ♦ SIR BENNI MILES ♦ PEOPLE NAMED 'TINY' ♦ GORE-TEX WITH THE KEY FOR THE SPIKES IN THE SOLE ♦ VIDEO MUSIC BOX ♦ GUESS? JEANS WITH THE PENCIL POCKET ♦ GUESS? JEANS WITH THE FARMERS POCKET ♦ TOMMY KNITS ♦ KING BEEF FROM MARTIN ♦ 8 BALL JACKETS (NOT THAT NEW SHIT THAT CAME OUT YEARS LATER WITH THE DIGITAL 8) ♦ MY 1ST GIG AS AN EXTRA VIA MY BIG SISTER WAS BEING IN THE MOVIE CLOCKERS, STICKY FINGAZ HAD THE ILLEST CB'34s ♦ MARK GRIFFITH AND THE CENTRAL BROOKLYN CREDIT UNION ♦ NAME PLATE EARRINGS ♦ HEAVY DUTY FROM G.I. JOE ♦ UPPER DECK BASEBALL CARDS ♦ TOPPS BASKETBALL CARDS ♦ DAS EFX ♦ BEAST FROM THE LAST DRAGON ♦ FRENCH TOAST (THE CLOTHES AND THE TASTY BREAKFAST) ♦ LIFESTYLES BEFORE MAGNUMS TOOK OVER ♦ THE PURPLE TAPE ♦ DJ CLUE MIXTAPES ♦ BAG HATS ♦ BABY HATS ♦ THE DUMB ASS KIDS WHO TOOK IT TOO FAR AND ACTUALLY SUCKED ON PACIFIERS ♦ CROOKED ICED TEA BEFORE THE 99 CENT ARIZONA TALL CAN ♦ NUMBER HOLES ♦ FU-SCHNICKENS ♦ 10 DOLLAR DRESSES ♦ COLUMBIA JACKETS WITH THE NAME (RAZZ-MATAZZ) ♦ LO HEADS BEFORE THE BERG HIT ♦ FRUSEN GLADJE BEFORE HAAGEN DAZ ♦ THE PENNY CANDLE STORE ♦ MISTER SOFTEE ICE CREAM TRUCKS ♦

MR. COOL ICE CREAM TRUCKS ♦ MAGIC MAN ICE CREAM TRUCKS ♦ MECCA JEANS ♦ MEDINA WARRIORS ♦ SHOW & PROVE ♦ ASICS ♦ AVIA 880 ♦ GIL NOBLE - LIKE IT IS (MOM WOULDN'T LET US CHANGE THE CHANNEL, VERY EDUCATIONAL BUT STILL BORING FOR PRETEENS) ♦ THE FUGEES ♦ THE FUGEES CHINESE RESTAURANT SKITS ♦ VANITY FROM LAST DRAGON ♦ VANITY FROM LAST DRAGON ♦ THE OLD BLACK AND WHITE SCHOOL CLOCKS WITH THE RED SECONDS HAND ♦ VANITY…FROM…LAST…DRAGON (WE LOVED HER…RIP) ♦ 40 ACRES & A MULE CLOTHING ♦ HERRINGBONES ♦ FOUR CHICKEN WINGS AND FRIED RICE ♦ CHICKEN PATTY WITH CHEESE AND COCO BREAD (I DIDN'T EAT BEEF) ♦ FINGER POPPIN AND TIDDY FUCKIN BEFORE BLOW JOBS AND ANAL WERE THE NORM ♦ GUN BARREL WATCHES ♦ DONNA KARAN ♦ YELLOW NUMBER 2 PENCILS WITH BOARD OF EDUCATION IN METALLIC GREEN ♦ DJEMBES ♦ HOMEMADE DASHIKIS ♦ SOUL GLOW ♦ CONNIE CHUNG ♦ WING CHUN ♦ LIQUID SWORDS ♦ CAPOEIRA ♦ BON TON POTATO CHIPS BEFORE UTZ ♦ ETONICS ♦ GIRLS PLAYING DOUBLE DUTCH WITH TELEPHONE WIRE ♦ BELL ATLANTIC PAY PHONES ♦ TROPICAL FANTASY 50 CENT SODAS (PEOPLE THOUGHT THEY MADE THE HOOD STERILE. THE BABIES CALL B.S. ON THAT ONE, MAY HAVE HELPED THE DIABETES RATE THOUGH) ♦ CLEAR CRACK VIALS WITH COLORED CAPS ♦ BUTTER ROLLS ♦ FOOD STAMP BOOKLETS ♦ TALESPIN ♦ RANDALL CUNNINGHAM ♦ AL BUNDY ONCE SCORED FOUR TOUCHDOWNS IN A SINGLE GAME ♦ DEATH TRAP PARTIES ♦ BASHMENTS ♦ PAPI OR AIIKI FOR EVERY BODEGA ♦ COOGI ♦ PEPE JEANS ♦ YOUNG RUDY FROM THE HUXTABLES ♦ MCDONALDS MOON MAN ♦ MARTY MCFLY ♦ LOVE LETTERS ♦ MOOKIE BLAYLOCK ♦ HAROLD MINER ♦ TINA TURNER IN MAD MAX ♦ CHET FROM WEIRD SCIENCE ♦ PLAYING

MANHUNT AT NIGHT ♦ FREEZE TAG ♦ STEAL THE BACON ♦ SPADES ♦ CRAZY 8s ♦ SKELLY ♦ 21 OR UTAH DEPENDING ON THE BLOCK YOU WERE FROM ♦ PLAY WRESTLING ♦ CLICK-CLACKS ♦ STREET HAWK ♦ NEIGHBORHOOD GAME ROOMS ♦ THE BROWN DOG IN DUCK HUNT ♦ JUMPING JACKS FIRECRACKERS ♦ CHERRY BOMBS ♦ M-80'S ♦ TRAPPER KEEPERS ♦ THE STRINGS ON JANSPORTS ♦ THE ORANGE SUPER SOAKER WITH THE YELLOW BOTTLE ♦ GARBAGE PAIL KIDS ♦ LITE BRITE ♦ TOFUTTI ♦ BOLO FROM ENTER THE DRAGON ♦ THE BRUK UP ♦ THE SAYING "I'M TRYNA HIT SOME SKINS" ♦ THE LOST BOYS, MOBB DEEP, M.O.P. ♦ WU-TANG ♦ ONYX ♦ ANIME (RATED MATURE) ♦ BLOCK PARTIES ♦ WHOLE BLOCK WATER FIGHTS ♦ SUMMERTIME BBQs ♦ A QUARTER WATER, A BALLOON AND A RUBBER BAND MAKE A BEAN SHOOTER ♦ ACTION JACKSON ♦ FALCOR FROM THE NEVERENDING STORY ♦ CELLA DWELLAS ♦ FLATLINERZ ♦ FLAT SHOE LACES ♦ VOLTRON ♦ WU WEAR ♦ HI-TEC BOOTS ♦ THE FIVE HEARTBEATS (NIGHTS LIKE THIS, I WISH, RAINDROPS WOULD FALL-AALL) ♦ THE TWO GRUMPY OLD MEN FROM THE MUPPETS ♦ BUSTER BROWN SHOE STORE ♦ CHICK-O-STICKS ♦ G.R.I.M. (SUPER INNER CIRCLE) ♦ STARTER SWEATSHIRTS ♦ INITIAL RINGS ♦ BO JACKSON ♦ RAZOR RUDDOCK ♦ GORTON'S FISH STICKS ♦ "I REMEMBER WHEN" STORIES ♦ SLAP BOXING ♦ DWAYNE WAYNE GLASSES ♦ THE ORANGE STATION INDICATOR ON OLD RADIOS ♦ GARGAMEL ♦ ALF ♦ TEDDY RUXPIN ♦ SARAFINA ♦ CROSS COLORS ♦ CRISS CROSS ♦ ROBIN GIVENS IN RAGE IN HARLEM ♦ HALLE BERRY IN BOOMERANG ♦ CREEPY CRAWLERS ♦ R.L. STINE'S GOOSEBUMPS ♦ CASPER FROM THE MOVIE KIDS ♦ SMALL LUTHER ♦ BIG OPRAH ♦ SMALL OPRAH ♦ BLACK MICHAEL ♦ WHITE MICHAEL ♦ DOUBLE RL ♦ DANGER MOUSE ♦ JACKIE JOYNER KERSEE ♦ DOLOMITES ♦ MONTHLY HOLOGRAMS ON

THE METRO PASS ♦ KARL KANI ♦ MAURICE MALONE ♦ FREAKAZOID! ♦ CAPTAIN CAVEMAN ♦ KID ICARUS ♦ GIZMODUCK ♦ FOZZIE FROM THE MUPPET BABIES ♦ THE WORD "BUTTER" ♦ HOWIE MANDEL AS BOBBY IN BOBBY'S WORLD ♦ TWO SCOOPS FROM AMERICAN GLADIATORS (THE 1ST AIRING) ♦ DICK GREGORY ♦ THE READING RAINBOW ♦ CRASH BANDICOOT ♦ 7 OF 9 FROM STAR TREK VOYAGER ♦ THE MIDGET HOOKER IN TOTAL RECALL ♦ BENNY THE CABBIE WITH THE ROACH ARM FROM TOTAL RECALL ♦ "OPEN YOUR MIND QUAID" ♦ ACTION JACKSON ♦ 1996 OLYMPICS ATLANTA ♦ FRIENDSHIP BRACELETS (GIRLS OF COURSE) ♦ MASK-THE ONE WITH CHER NOT JIM CARREY ♦ THE 'THESE PEOPLE' SECTION FROM THE ARSENIO HALL SHOW ♦ JAWBREAKERS ♦ ORCA ♦ RICHARD BEY BEFORE JERRY SPRINGER ♦ DECEPTICONS ♦ FRESH OTIS SPUNKMEYER COOKIE BEFORE FAMOUS AMOS ♦ APARTHEID ♦ APPLE CIDER ♦ CLOGS ♦ JELLYS ♦ CHINESE SLIPPERS ♦ THOSE FAST LONG BROWN FRAIL CENTIPEDE LOOKING THINGS-WE CALLED THEM SPIDER ROACHES (SILVERFISH) ♦ MYRA FROM FAMILY MATTERS (RIP) ♦ BAZOOKA GUM COMIC STRIPS IN THE WRAPPER ♦ KOKO B. WARE ♦ STAYING UP TILL DAYBREAK ♦ NUMBER MUNCHERS (THE COMPUTER GAME) ♦ FLEX AND THE UPTOWN COMEDY CLUB ♦ THE THIGHMASTER (MOMS HAD ONE) ♦ "I BUST STUPID DOPE MOVES" ♦ TOMMY FROM POWER RANGERS ♦ HALLOWEEN EGG FIGHTS ♦ VIPER CAR ALARMS ♦ BOX CUTTERS ♦ GEMSTAR ♦ GAME GENIE FOR STREET FIGHTER (YOU COULD THROW MULTIPLE HADOUKENS. AND A TATA-UUUKENS BEFORE YOU HIT THE GROUND, THAT WAS AMAZING) ♦ LARRY JOHNSON, GRANDMAMA ♦ SCHOOL DAZE - "YOU GAVE IT UP TO HALF PINT, OHH JANE" ♦ PAUL FROM WONDER YEARS ♦ VICKY FROM SMALL WONDER ♦ AUSARA SET ♦ FARMERS MARKETS ♦ BIRTHDAY

PUNCHES ♦ ACID WASH JEANS (I STILL HAVE A PAIR IN THE CLOSET) ♦ P.A.L. BASKETBALL ♦ JODECI, BOYZ TO MEN, SWV ♦ GINGER ALE WHEN IT ACTUALLY HAD GINGER IN IT ♦ TWO DOLLAR BILLS (THEY WERE NEVER DISCONTINUED) ♦ CLASSROOM PIZZA PARTIES ♦ HOUSE PARTIES WITH THE WEIRD FAMILY MEMBER ♦ JAW SWINGERS, GREAT MINDZ, U.N.I.SIN (INNER CIRCLE) ♦ MAMA'S FRIED, CROWN FRIED, KENNEDY FRIED CHICKEN ♦ ANY COIN WITH YOUR BIRTH YEAR ♦ PATTIE, ARETHA, CHAKA ♦ WEARING SOCKS OVER THE CUFF OF YOUR JEANS, ONLY IN THE BACK ♦ BEENIE MAN, ELEPHANT MAN, BOUNTY KILLER ♦ MILK CRATE BASKETBALL RIMS ♦ LIVE 95 ♦ PARASUCOS ♦ BUSTA, ODB, BIG, JAY ♦ S&D'S ♦ MUG ROOT BEER ♦ EVERY DESIGNER MADE A JUMPER ♦ PERRY ELLIS ♦ GINSENG UP SODA ♦ TURBOGRAFX 16 ♦ WIFFLE BALL ON THE SIDEWALK ♦ NEO GEO ♦ THREE SECOND HOLD ♦ PREGNANT STREET CATS ♦ THE NOSEY NEIGHBOR ♦ THE NEIGHBORHOOD SMUT ♦ THE NEIGHBORHOOD ALKY ♦ CRACKHEADS YOU KNEW PERSONALLY AND THE CONVERSATIONS YOU HAD WITH THEM FOR YOUR ENTERTAINMENT ♦ LEE, LEVI'S, JORDACHE JEANS ♦ WE WORE VISORS IN THE SUMMER ♦ FRAGGLE ROCK ♦ SCRUFF MCGRUFF ♦ SMOKEY THE BEAR ♦ YOGI BEAR AND THE SWISS CHEESE BUS THAT CAME ON YOUR BLOCK AND TOOK YOUR ASS TO SOME WEIRD HOOD DAY CAMP EVERY SATURDAY DURING THE SUMMER (I ONLY WENT ONCE) ♦ FREE SUMMER SCHOOL LUNCH (I WENT TWICE, WE WERE HUNGRY) ♦ DOOGIE HOWSER JOURNALS BEFORE SARAH JESSICA PARKER ♦ LOU DIAMOND PHILLIPS ♦ SUPER CAT, CAPLETON, WARRIOR KING, SIZZLA, BUJU ♦ DICK TRACEY ♦ TOPANGA ♦ SATURDAY AFTERNOON KUNG FU MARATHONS ♦
THE 99 CENT STORE WHEN MOST THINGS WERE 99 CENT ♦ ARMED AND DANGEROUS STRAIGHT UP WEED NO ANGEL DUST

(I NEVER SMOKED) ♦ THREE CUTS IN YOUR EYEBROWS TRYNA WILD OUT (I HAD ONE CUT) ♦ ALL CARS HAD LONG ANTENNAS ♦ CALCULATOR WATCHES ♦ THE ROOFTOP SCENE FROM JASON TAKES MANHATTAN ♦ G-MONEY ♦ NEW JERSEY DRIVE ♦ DIGABLE PLANETS ♦ LADY SAW ♦ THE BROTHER FROM ANOTHER PLANET ♦ SUN-MAN ♦ THE COLOR GREEN IN THE MOVIE THE WIZ ♦ LAURENCE FISHBURNE AS COWBOY IN PEE WEE'S PLAYHOUSE ♦ HOMEY D. CLOWN ♦ TRAIN CAR GRAFFITI ♦ SUMMER CRUSHES ♦ THE SAYING "WE GO TOGETHER" ♦ AS YOU CAN SEE, THIS LIST CAN GO ON AND ON. YOU CAN FILL IN THE REST……..ACTUALLY, CALL A FRIEND AND REMINISCE ABOUT YOUR CREDITS.

♦ THE BEST SNEAKERS CAME IN HIGH TOP ♦

www.ingramcontent.com/pod-product-compliance
Lightning Source LLC
Chambersburg PA
CBHW071401290426
44108CB00014B/1637